HOW TO DRAW WOODLAND CREATURES

for kids

ALLI KOCH

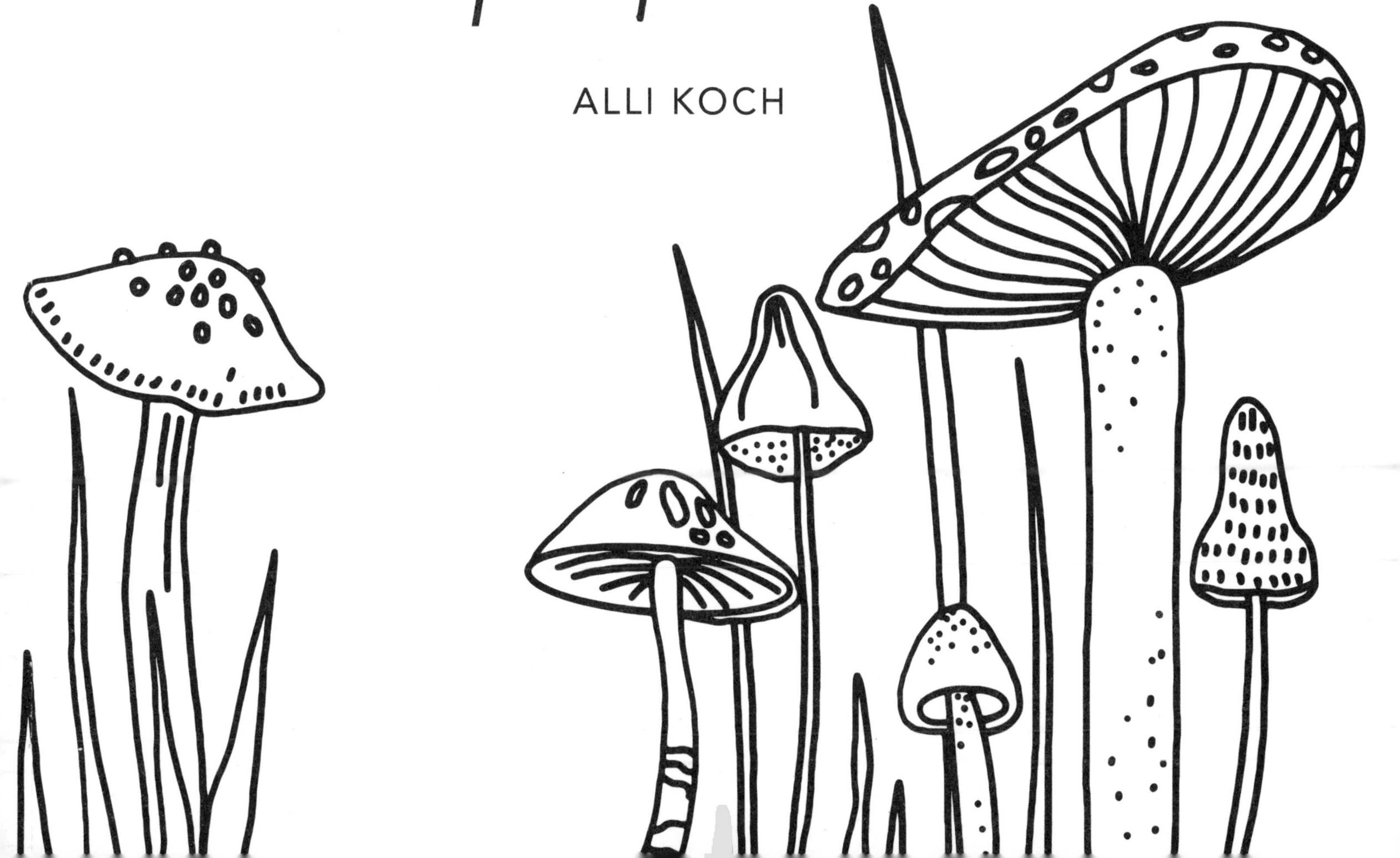

Paige Tate & Co.

Published by Blue Star Press

PO Box 8835, Bend, OR 97708

contact@bluestarpress.com

www.bluestarpress.com

Written and illustrated by Alli Koch

ISBN: 9781958803721

Printed in Colombia

10 9 8 7 6 5 4 3 2

this book
BELONGS TO

LET'S DRAW!

The nice thing about being an artist is that you can make the rules. Everyone has their own style, which is why your drawings will look different from someone else's. In this book, each woodland creature or plant is broken down into steps. My goal is to help you see the simple parts of what may seem like a hard thing to draw.

We will start with the most basic outline or guide and work our way up. You will start to see a pattern with each animal we draw, starting with simple guide lines, then breaking down "C" and "S" shape lines, and lastly erasing the unneeded lines for the finished look. Don't forget to draw your lines lightly first so it is easier to erase them. My favorite thing to say when drawing is:

If it was perfect, it would not look handmade!

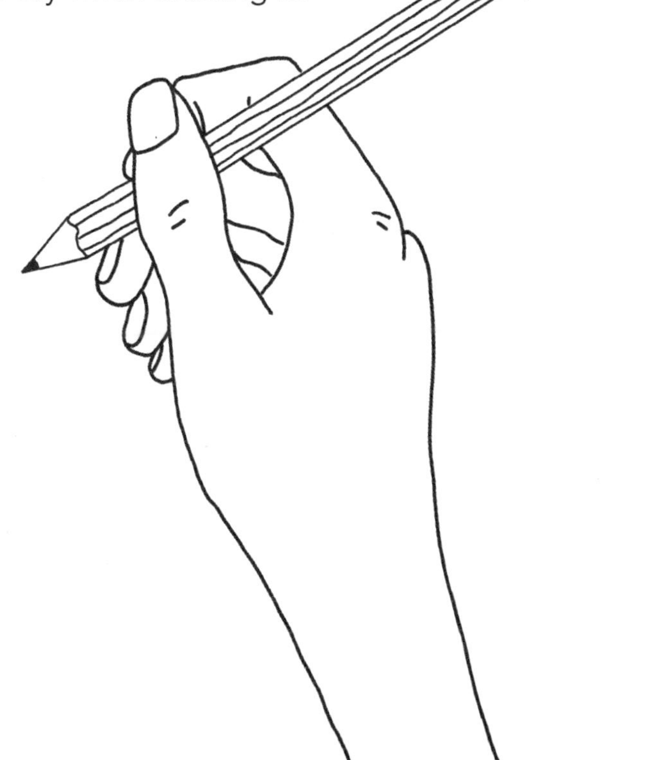

TOOLS

The cool thing about art is that you can use any tool you want! Yep, that's right! You are the artist, so feel free to be creative. For this book, let's keep it simple. It's easy to learn using either blank sheets of paper or grid paper.

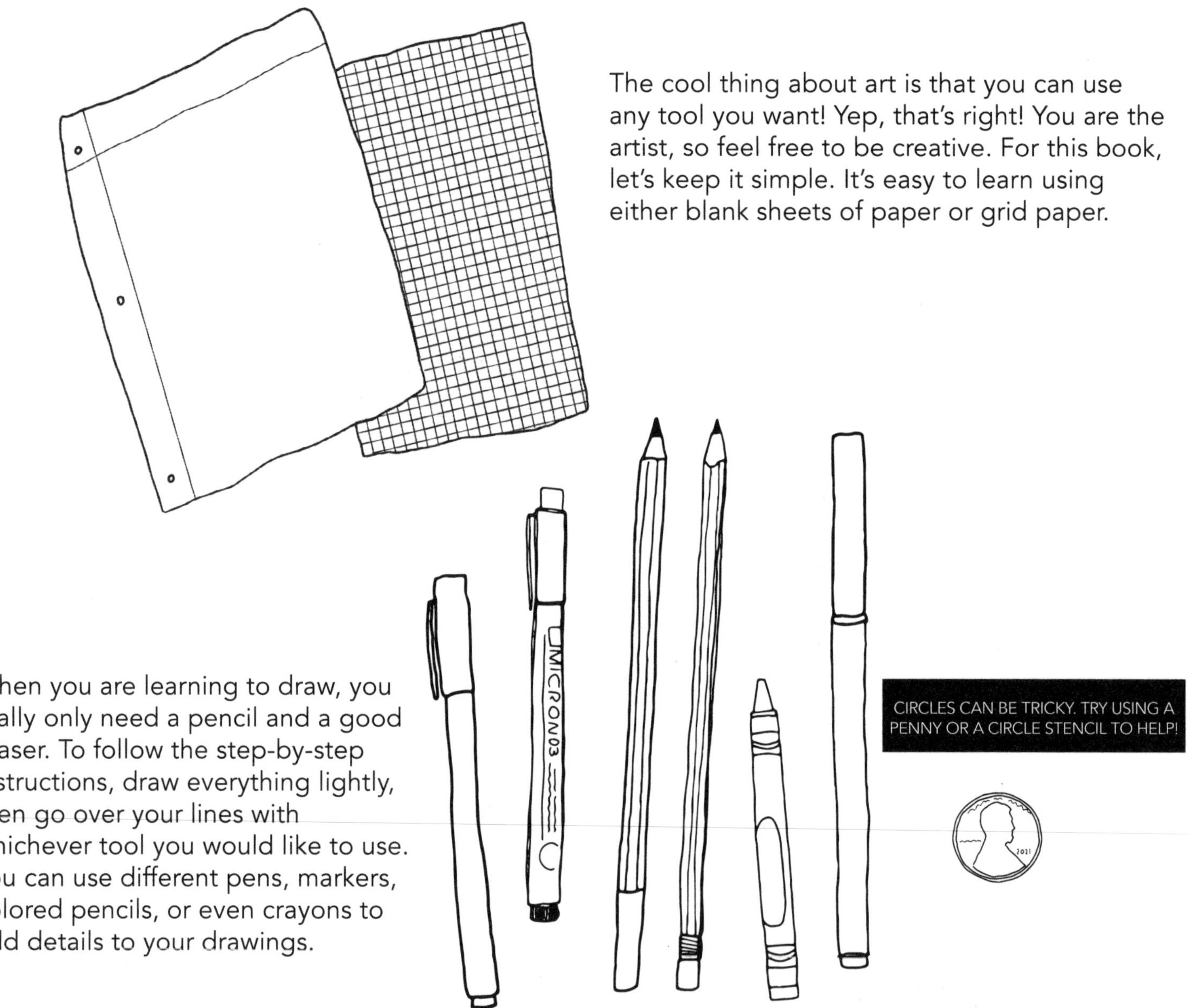

When you are learning to draw, you really only need a pencil and a good eraser. To follow the step-by-step instructions, draw everything lightly, then go over your lines with whichever tool you would like to use. You can use different pens, markers, colored pencils, or even crayons to add details to your drawings.

CIRCLES CAN BE TRICKY. TRY USING A PENNY OR A CIRCLE STENCIL TO HELP!

BREAK IT DOWN

Anyone can draw! If you can write your ABCs (which I am pretty sure you can do!), then you can draw everything in this book. Each animal or plant can be broken down into a bunch of "C" and "S" shaped lines. Almost anything that is round is two simple "C" lines put together. An "S" line is for when something has a dip or curvy line.

Most of the creatures in this book are broken down into six or eight steps. What you will draw in each step will be a black line; what you have already done will be in gray line. There are more than 60 projects in this book for you to learn how to draw. The chapter dividers in this book are also bonus coloring pages!

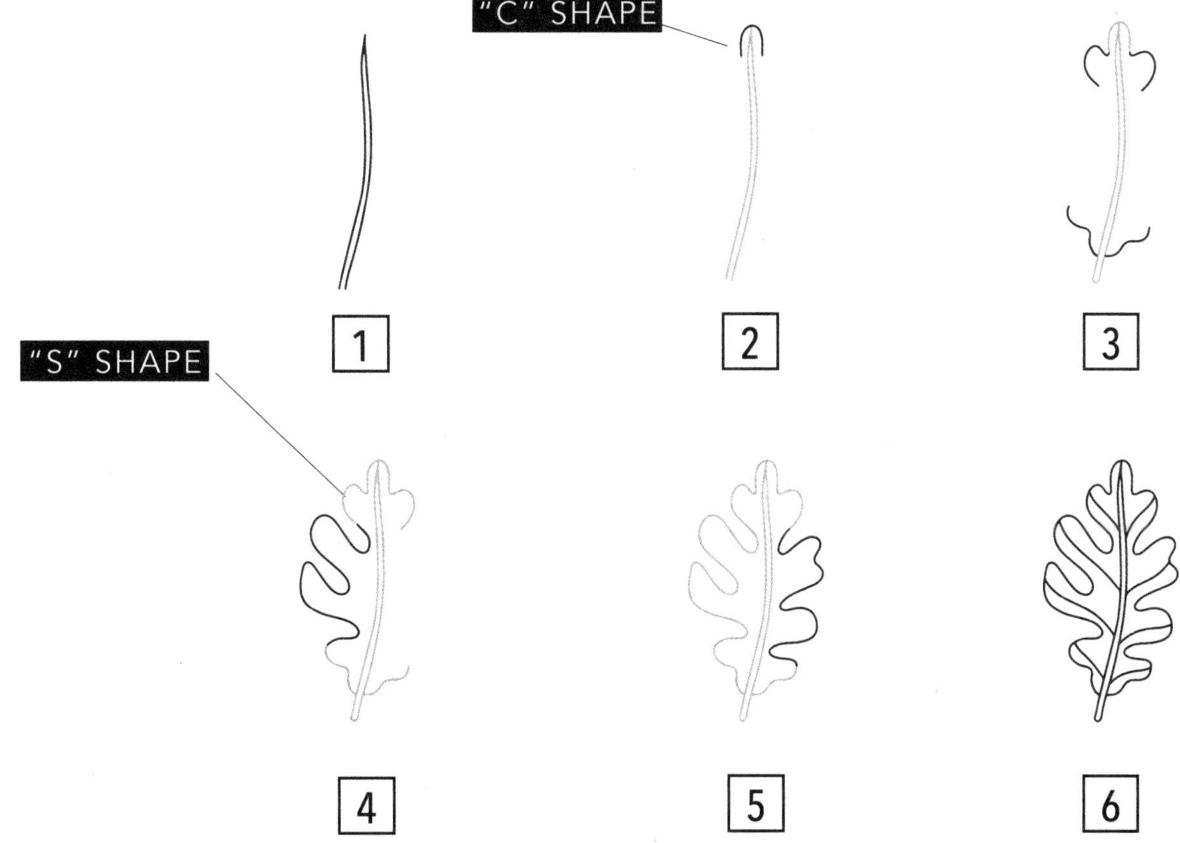

ANIMALS

RABBIT

Did you know that rabbits can become lonely? They're happiest when they have other rabbits to keep them company!

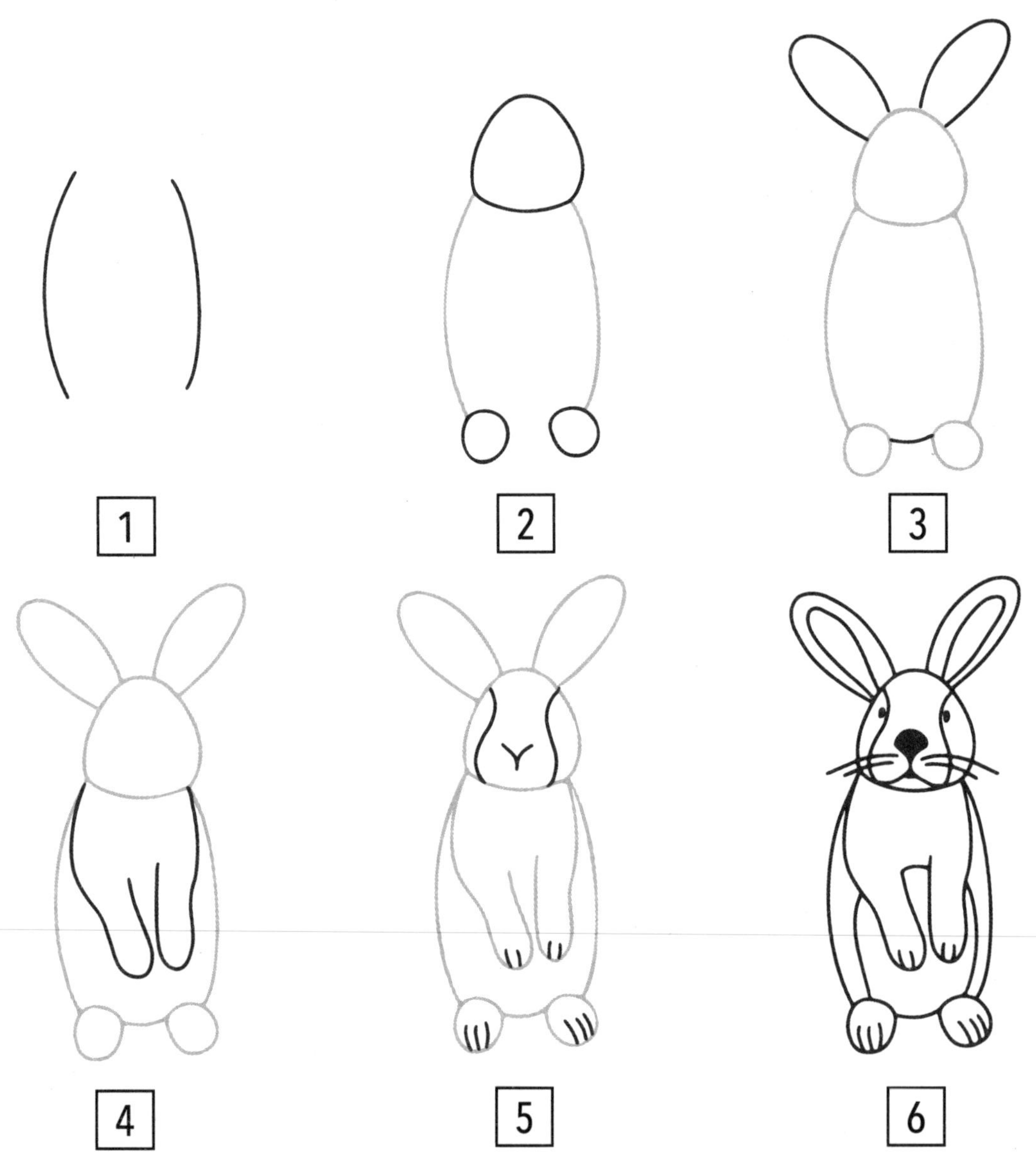

RACCOON

Raccoons love to eat wild berries, nuts, insects, and even trash left behind by humans.

MINK

Minks purr when they're happy—just like cats!

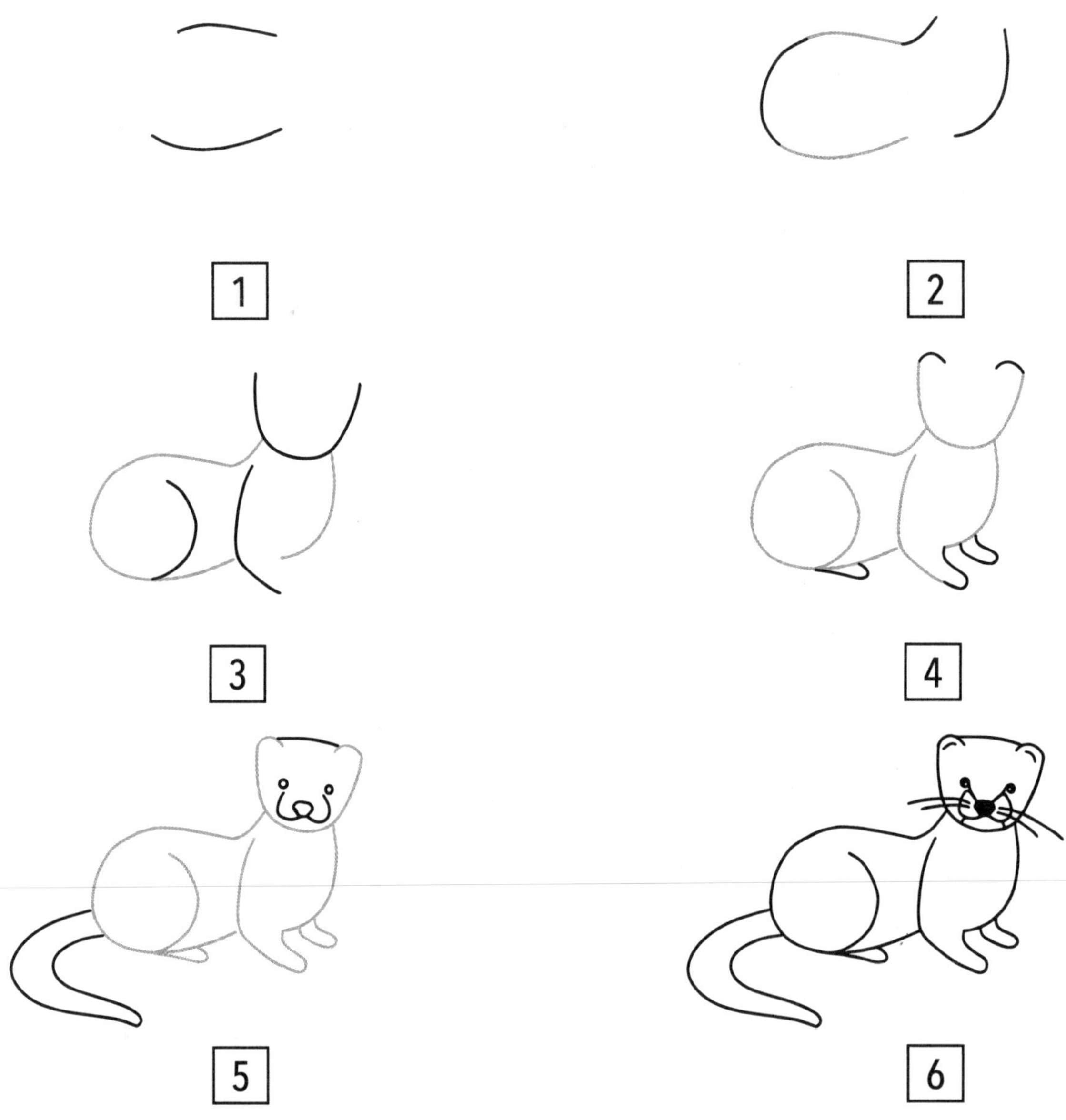

BEAR

There are 8 bear species in the world, 3 of which live in North America: brown bears, black bears, and polar bears.

DEER

If you see a deer with antlers, it's a male deer. Female deer, called doe, are unable to grow antlers.

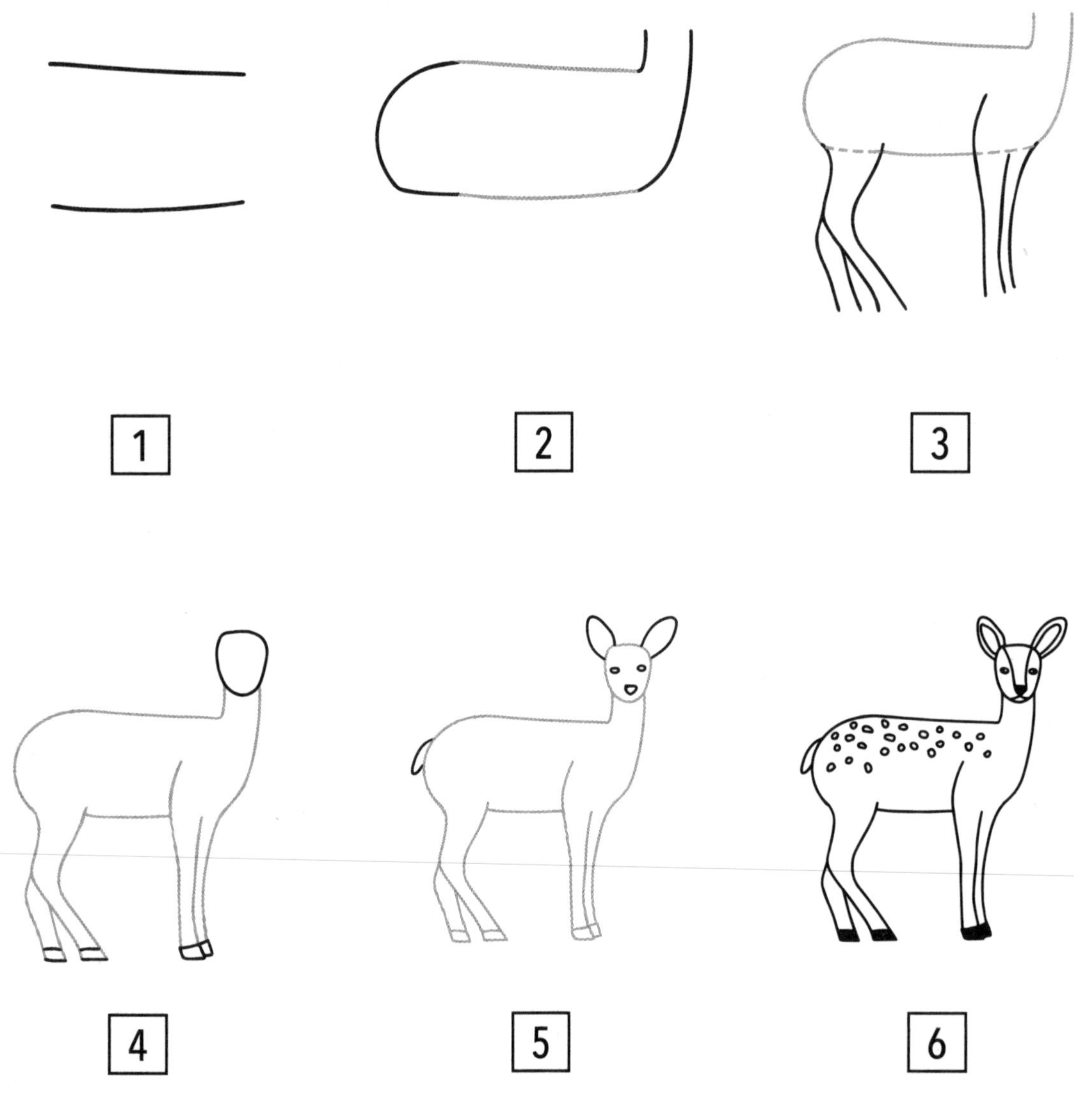

BASS

Bass can live to be 16 years old.

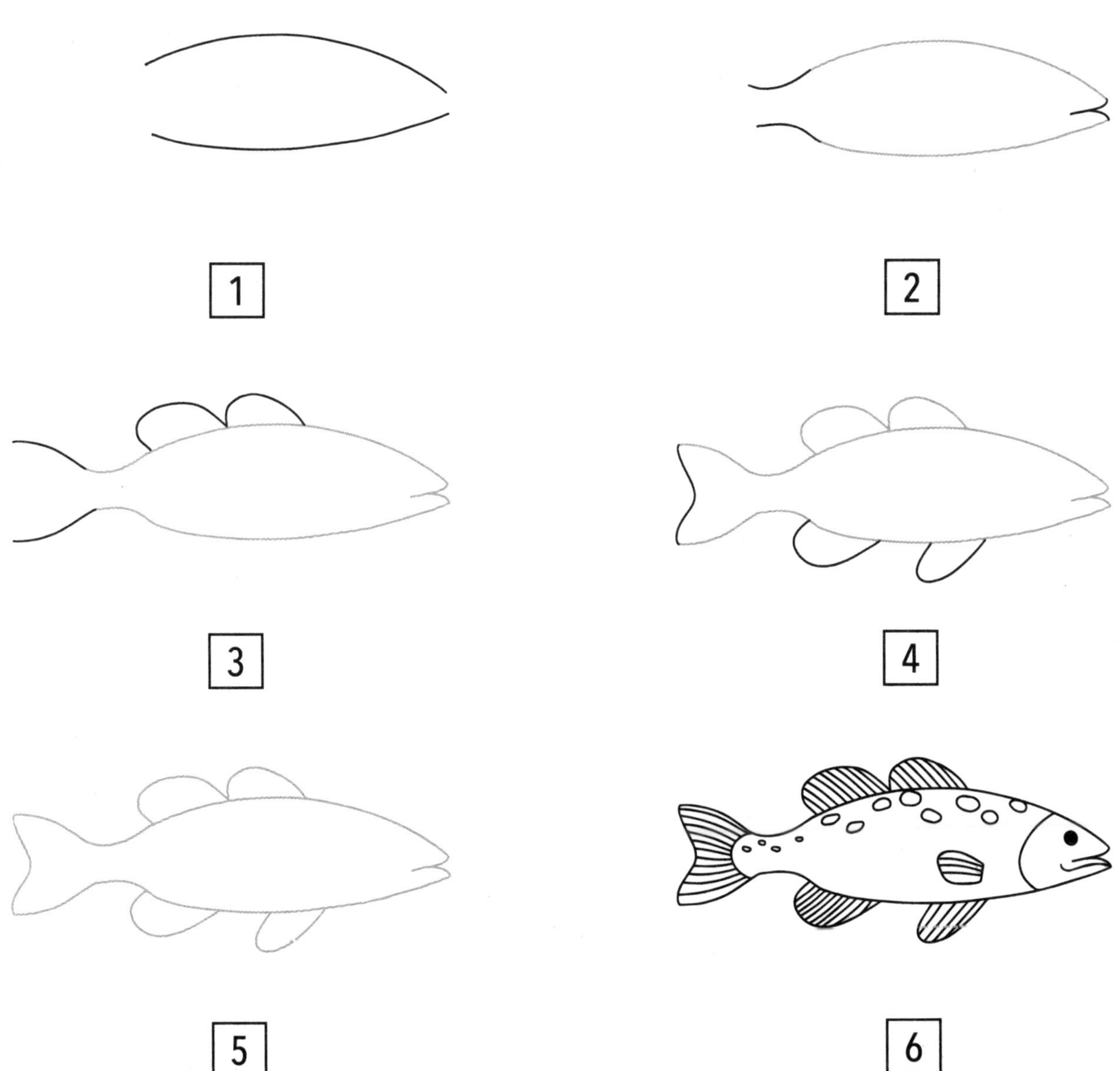

SQUIRREL

Squirrels love to eat! They can smell food buried beneath a foot of snow.

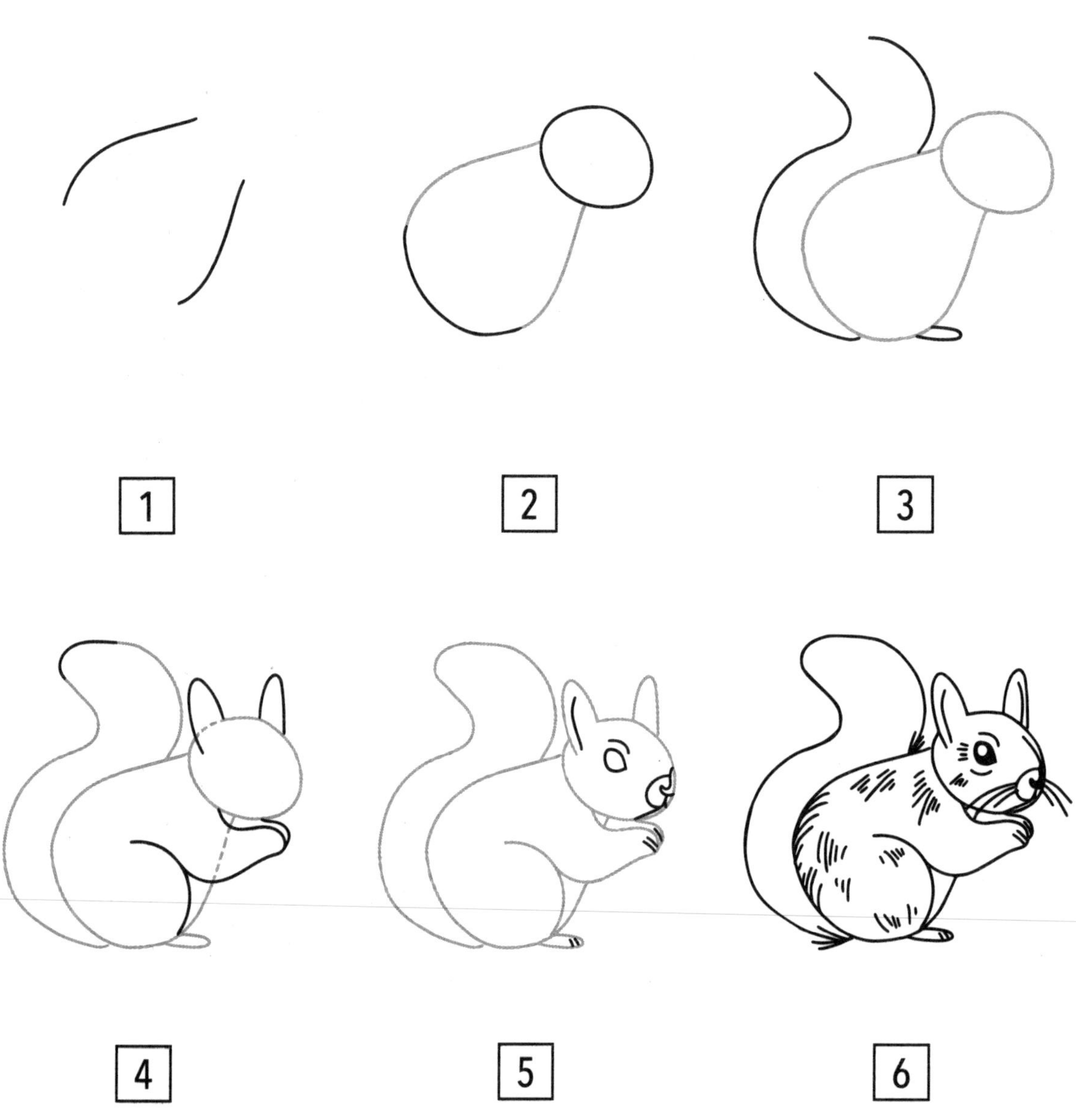

SKUNK

Once a skunk sprays its stinky odor on a predator, it takes 10 to 12 days to replenish their spray.

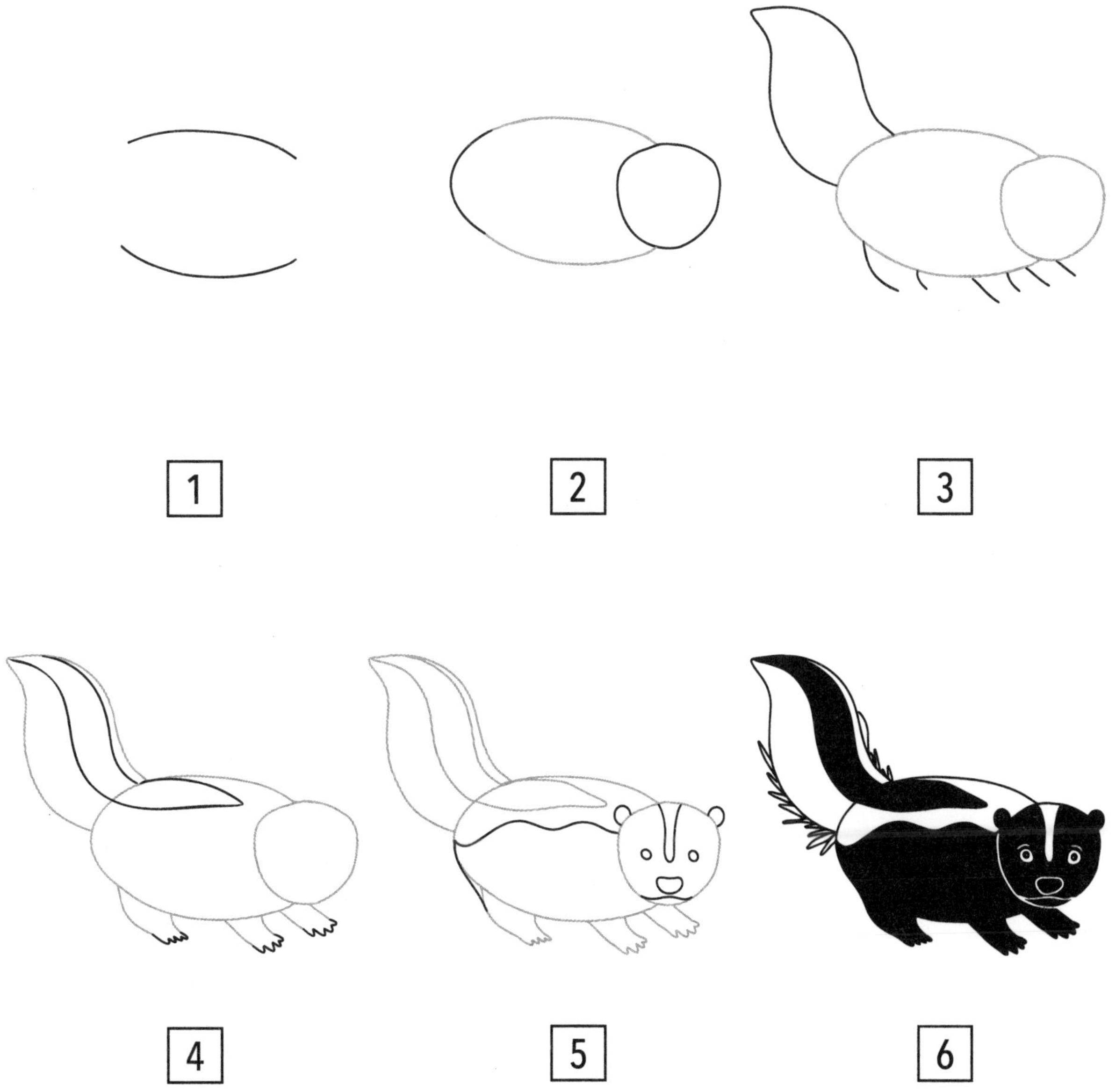

BEAVER

A beaver's teeth are always growing, and they have to gnaw on tree bark to keep their teeth short.

CHIPMUNK

A chipmunk can hold a stash of food in its cheeks that's 3 times the size of its head.

PORCUPINE

The North American porcupine has more than 30,000 sharp quills on its body!

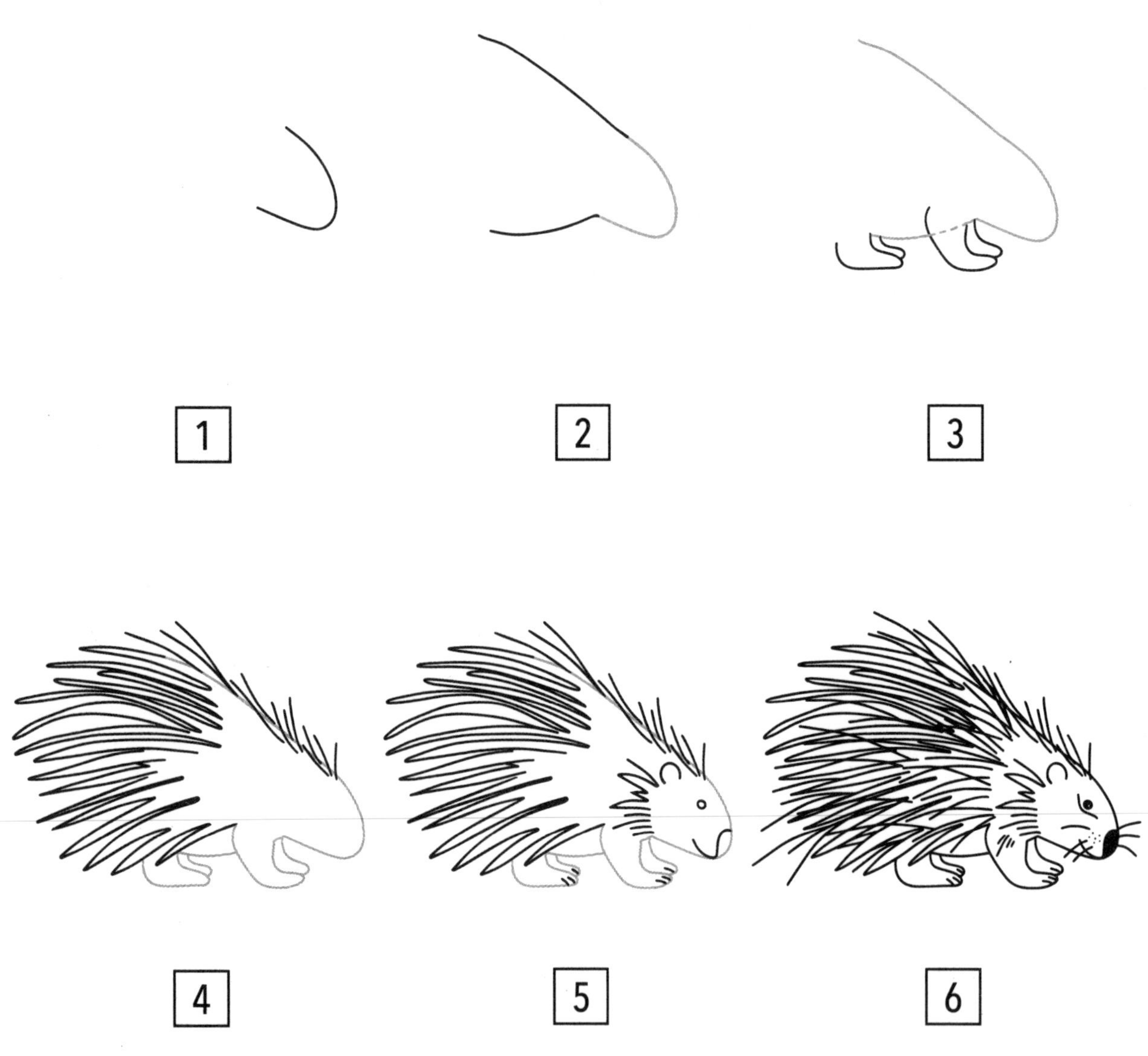

MOOSE

Moose are huge animals! An average adult moose weighs up to 1,500 pounds.

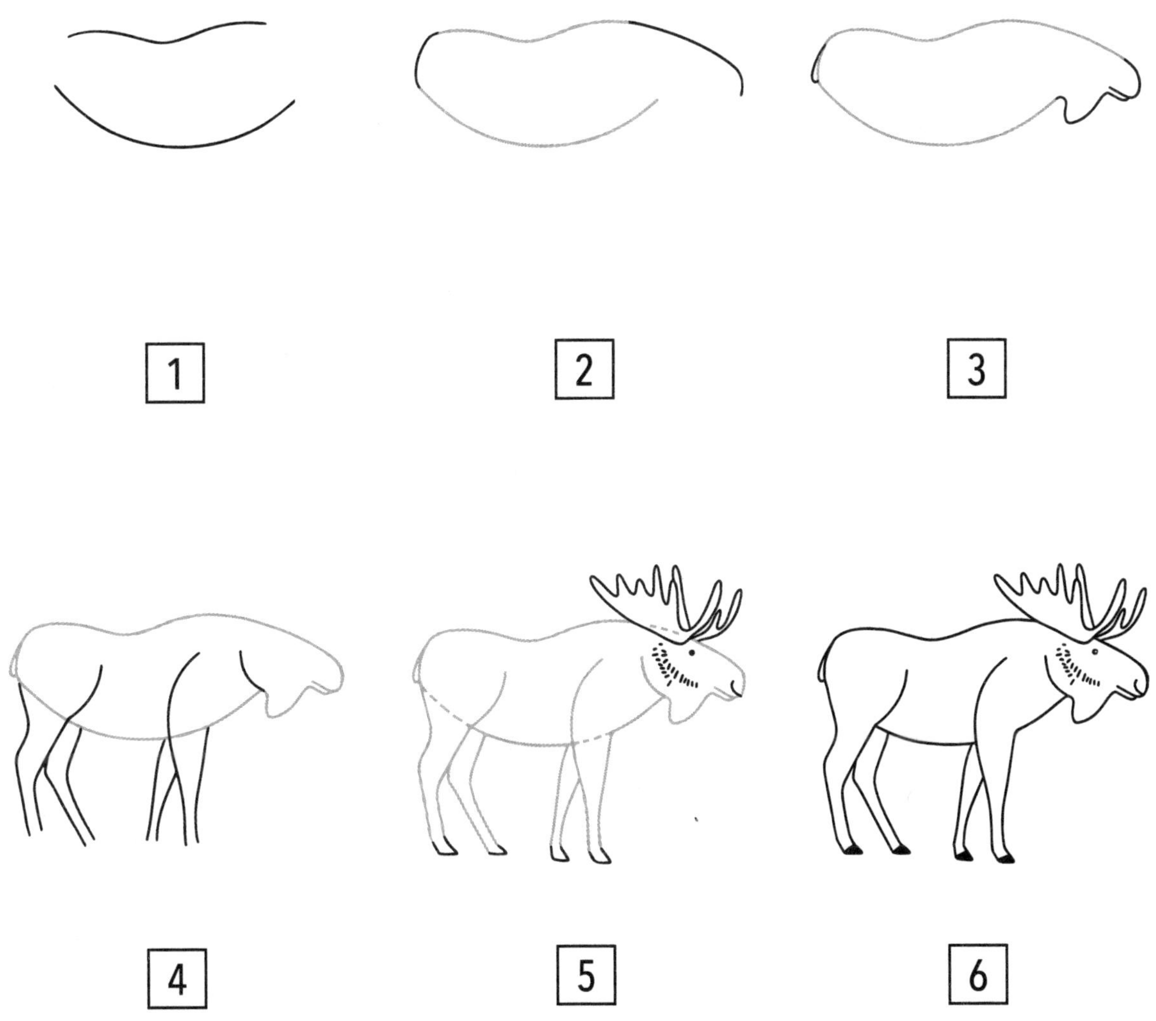

BOBCAT

These cats get their name from their very short tail, which appears to have been cut off or "bobbed."

1 2

3 4

5

6

7

8

TOAD

A group of toads is called a knot.

BADGER

A baby badger is called a cub, and a group of badgers is called a clan.

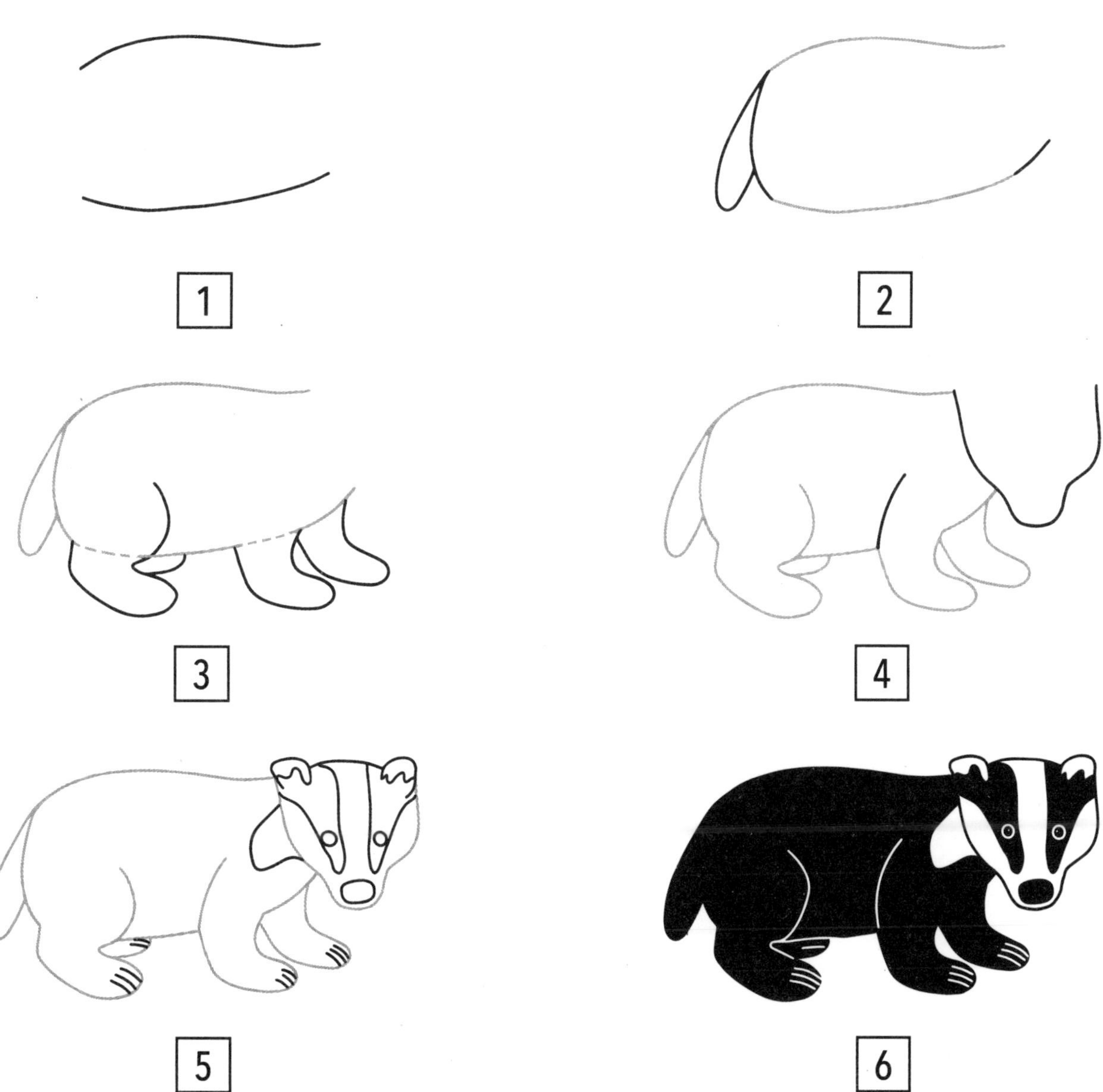

VOLE

Voles weigh just 2 ounces, but they can dig extensive tunnels underground. Some vole tunnels measure more than 100 feet in diameter.

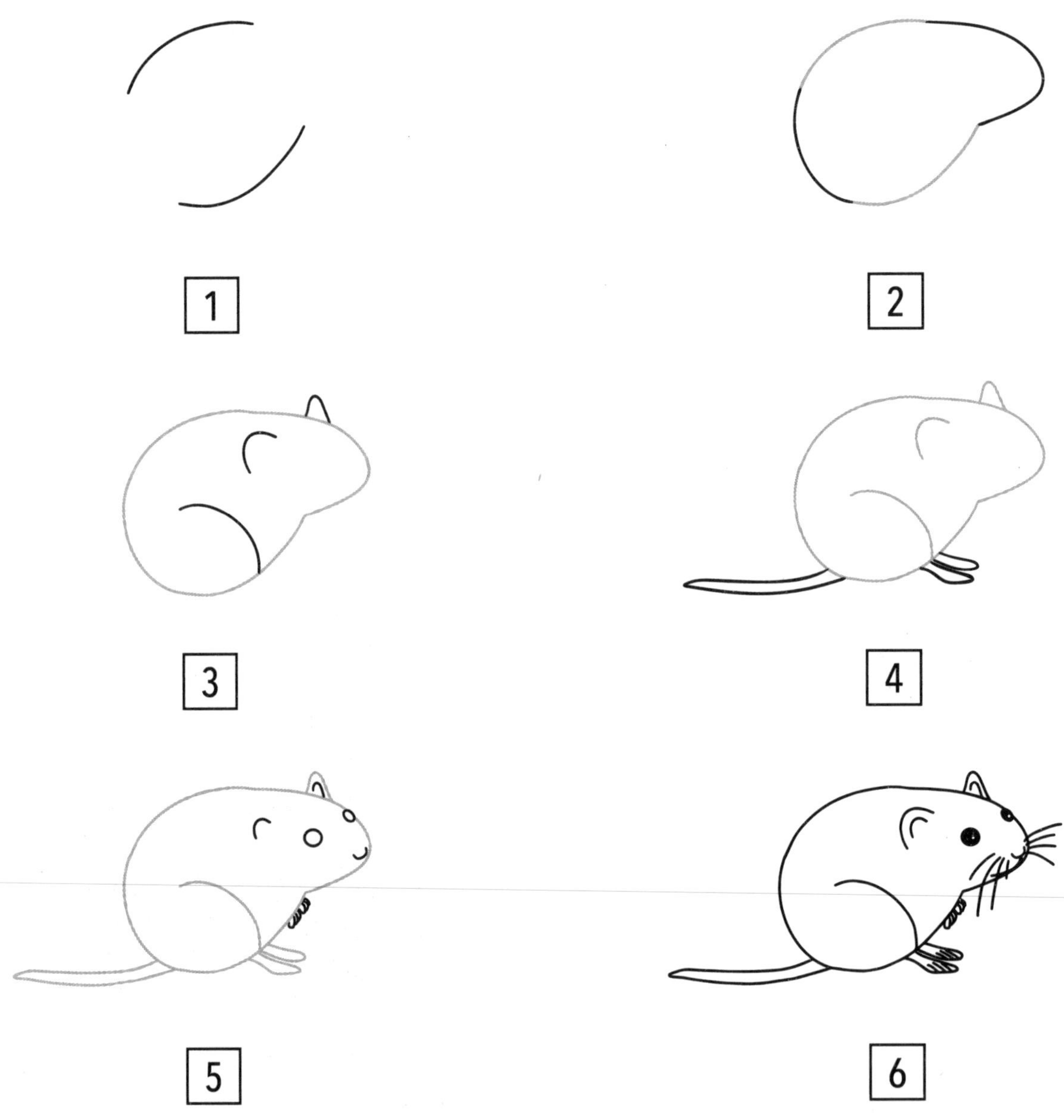

SNAKE

Snakes use their tongues to smell.

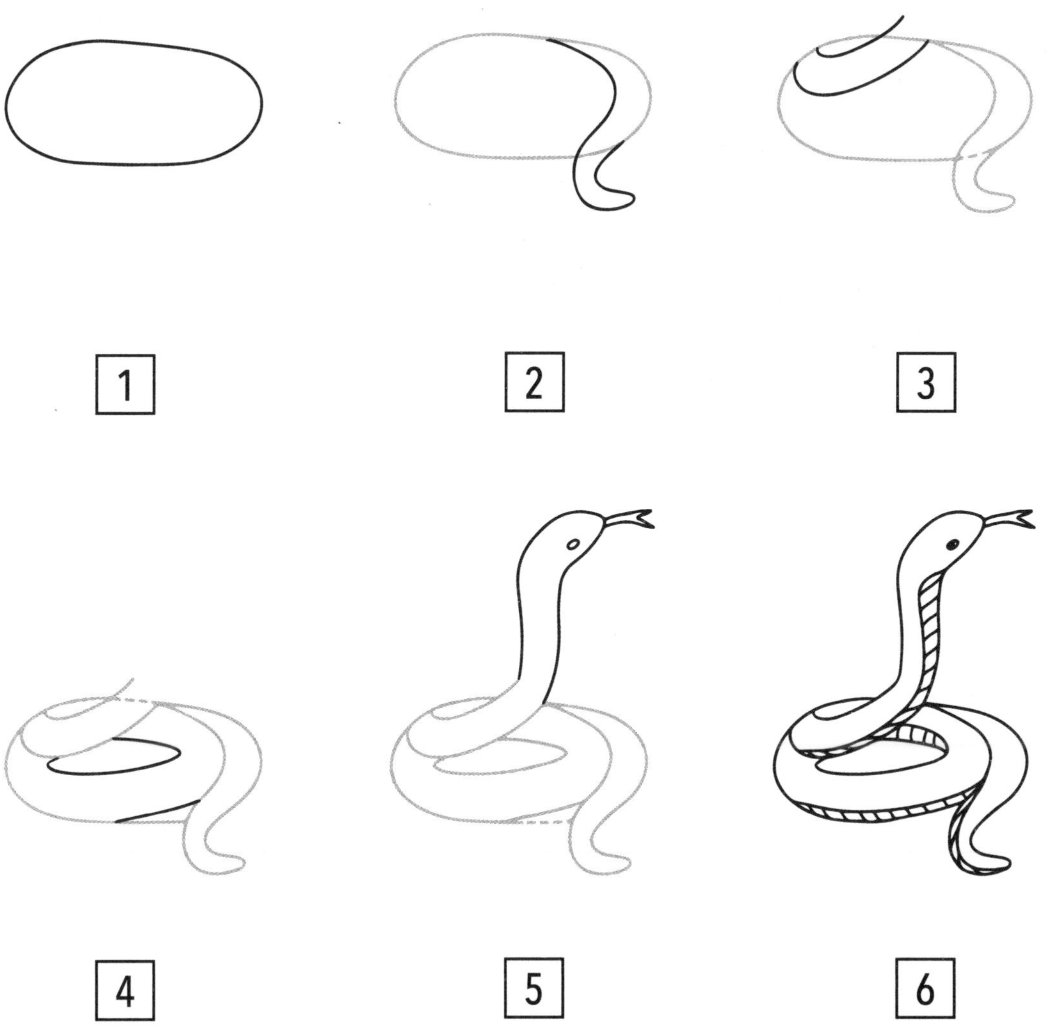

FOX

Foxes can see in the dark, which allows them to hunt at night.

1 2

3 4

5
6
7
8

HEDGEHOG

Hedgehogs got their name because they love to dig underneath garden hedges, and they make hog-like grunting sounds.

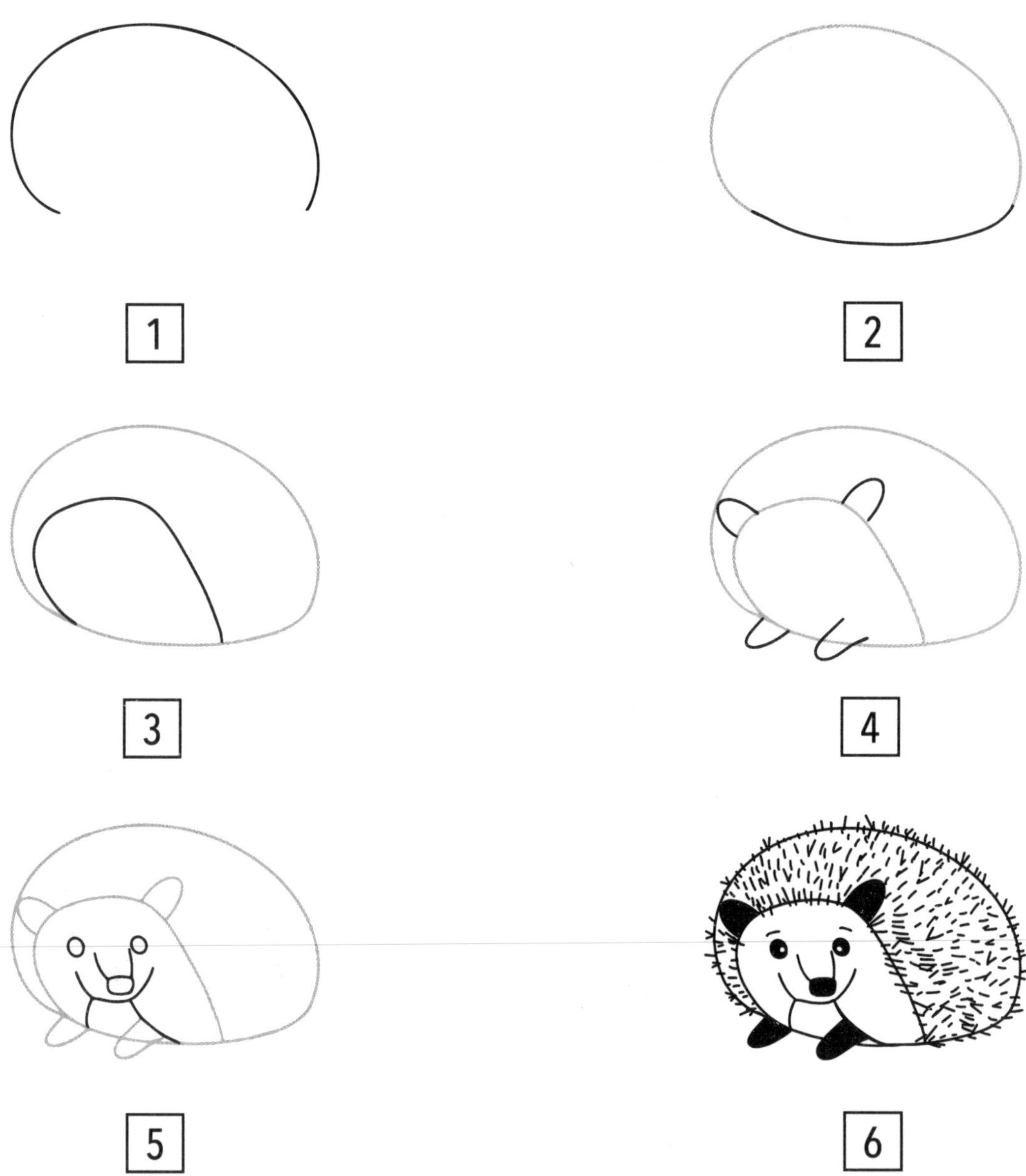

MOLE

Because they mainly eat worms and insects, moles have long claws that help them dig underground to find their next meal.

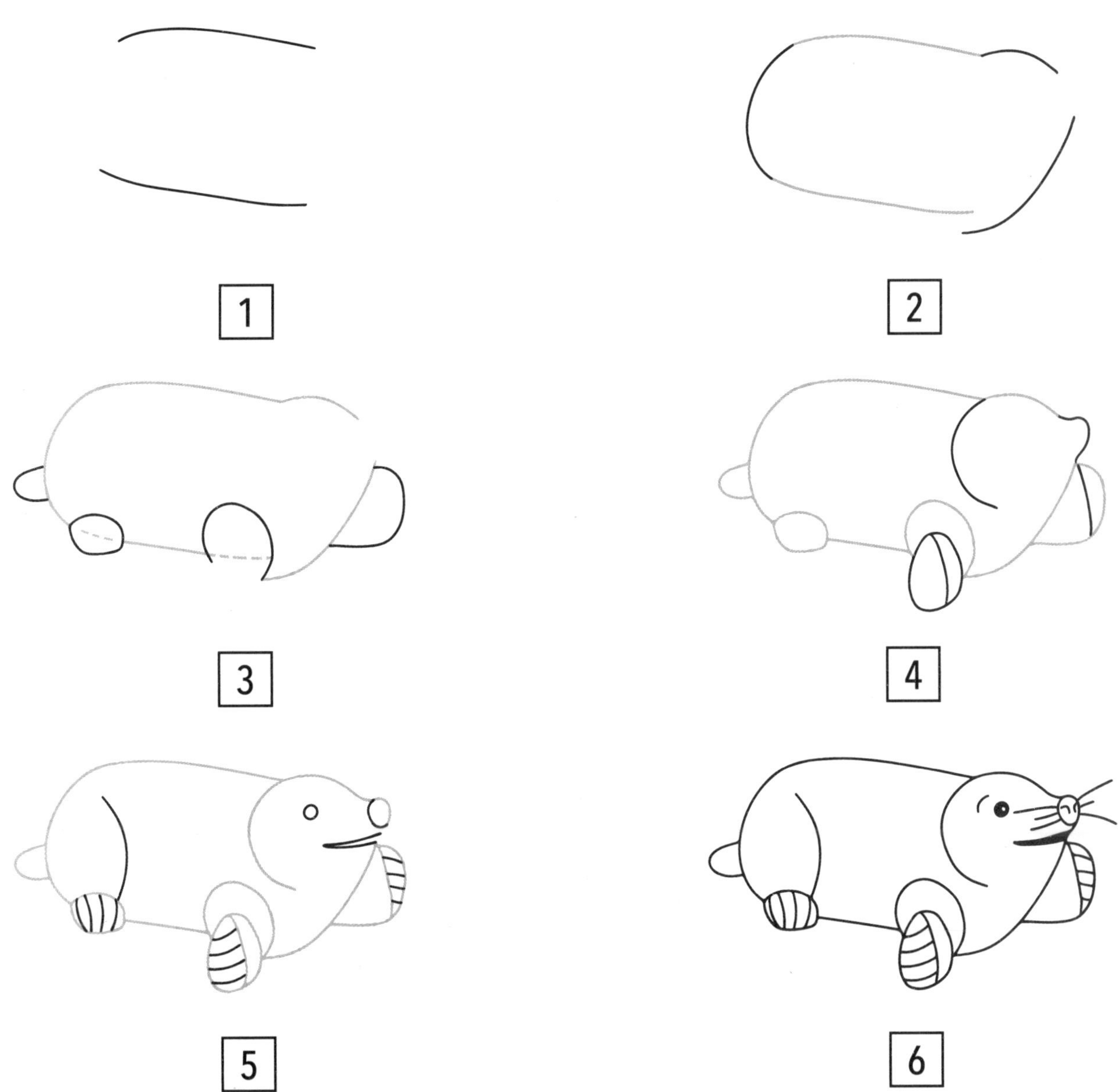

OPOSSUM

Often referred to as a "possum," an opossum will roll over and play dead when it feels threatened.

LIZARD

Some lizards can detach their tails to help them escape if they get caught by a predator.

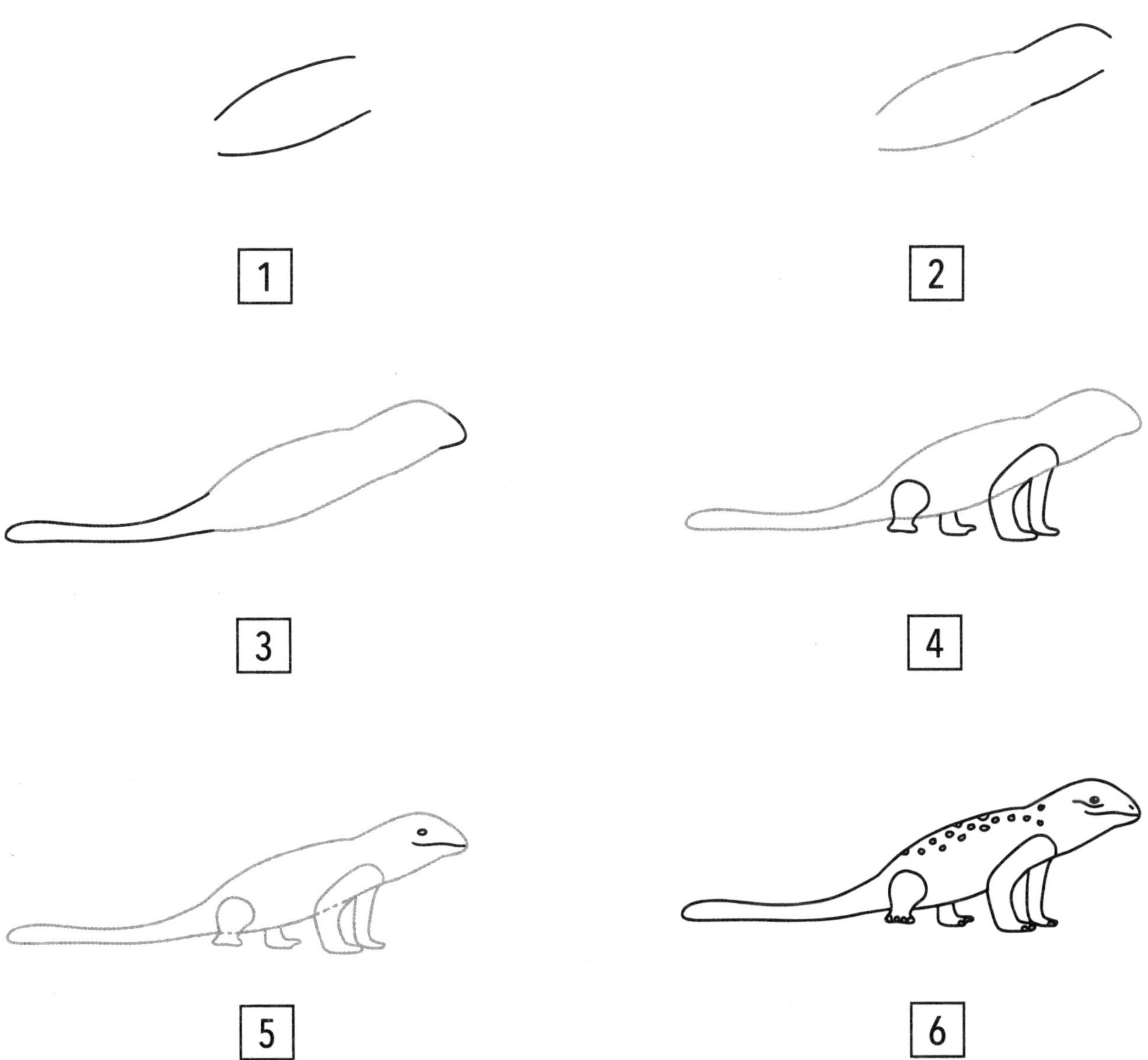

HOG

Hogs may not have great eyesight, but they can smell odors from 5–7 miles away.

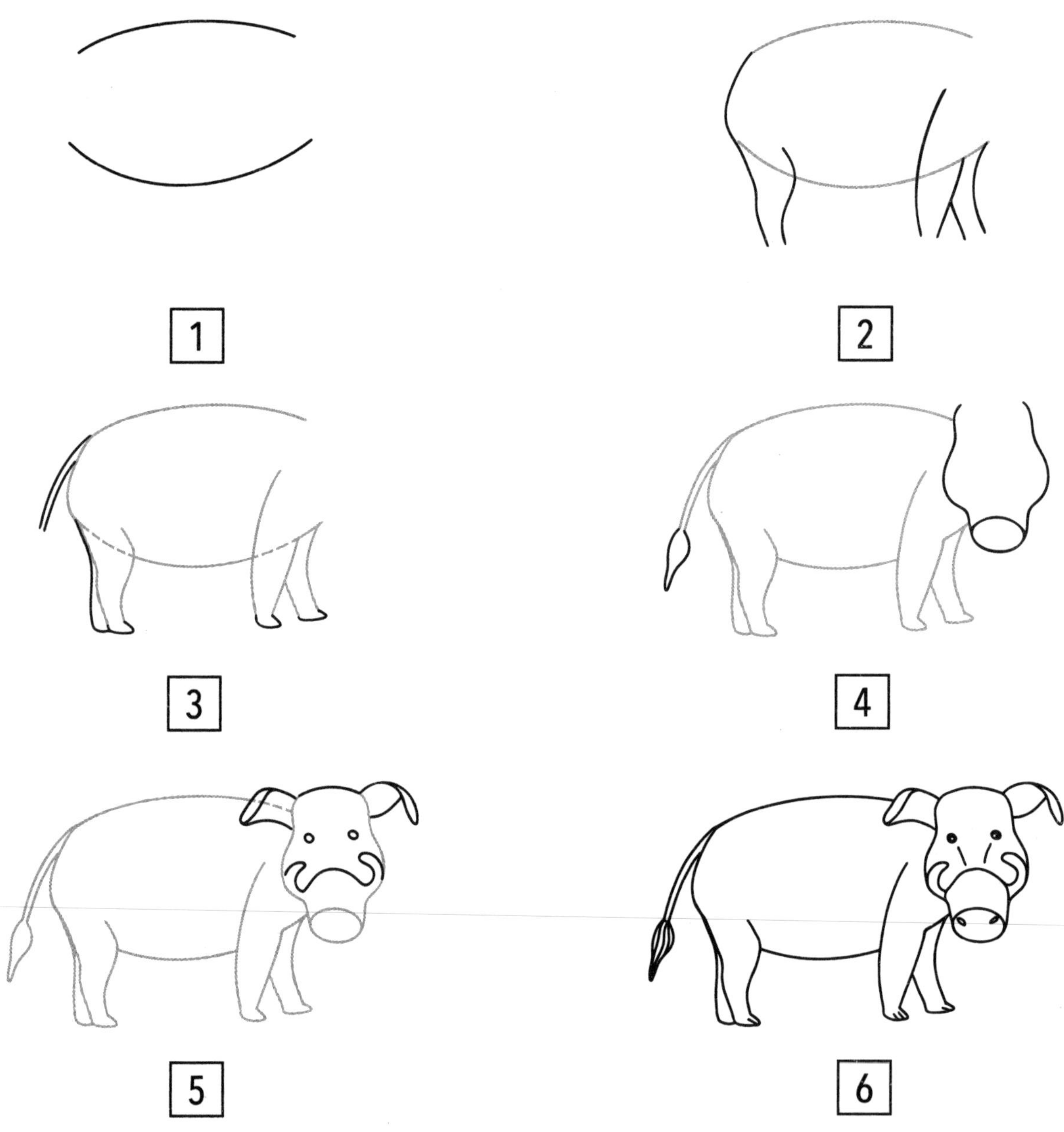

TURTLE

Turtles have been around for more than 200 million years, which means they existed alongside dinosaurs!

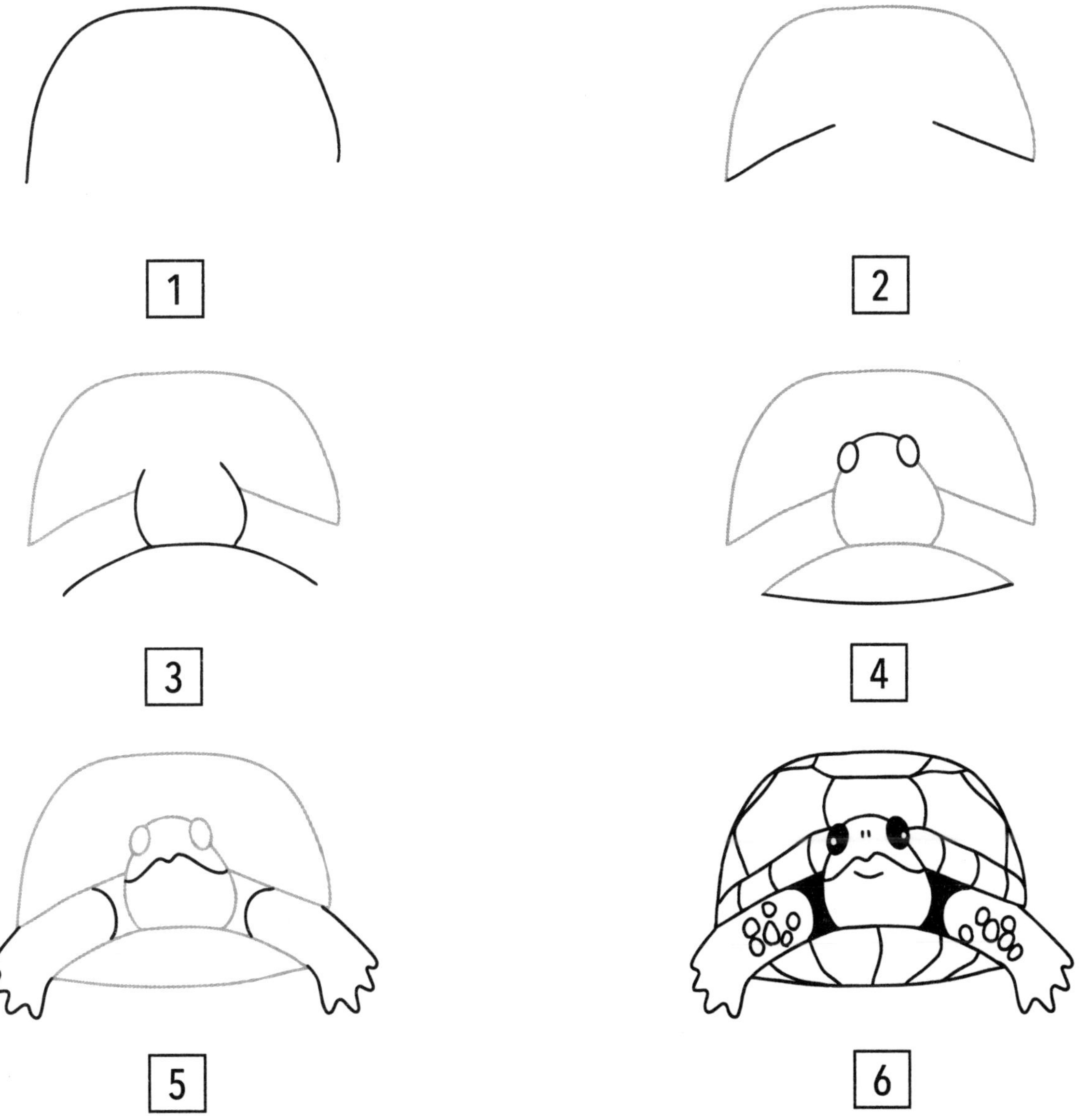

MUSKRAT

When they swim, muskrats use their webbed feet as paddles and their tails as little rudders.

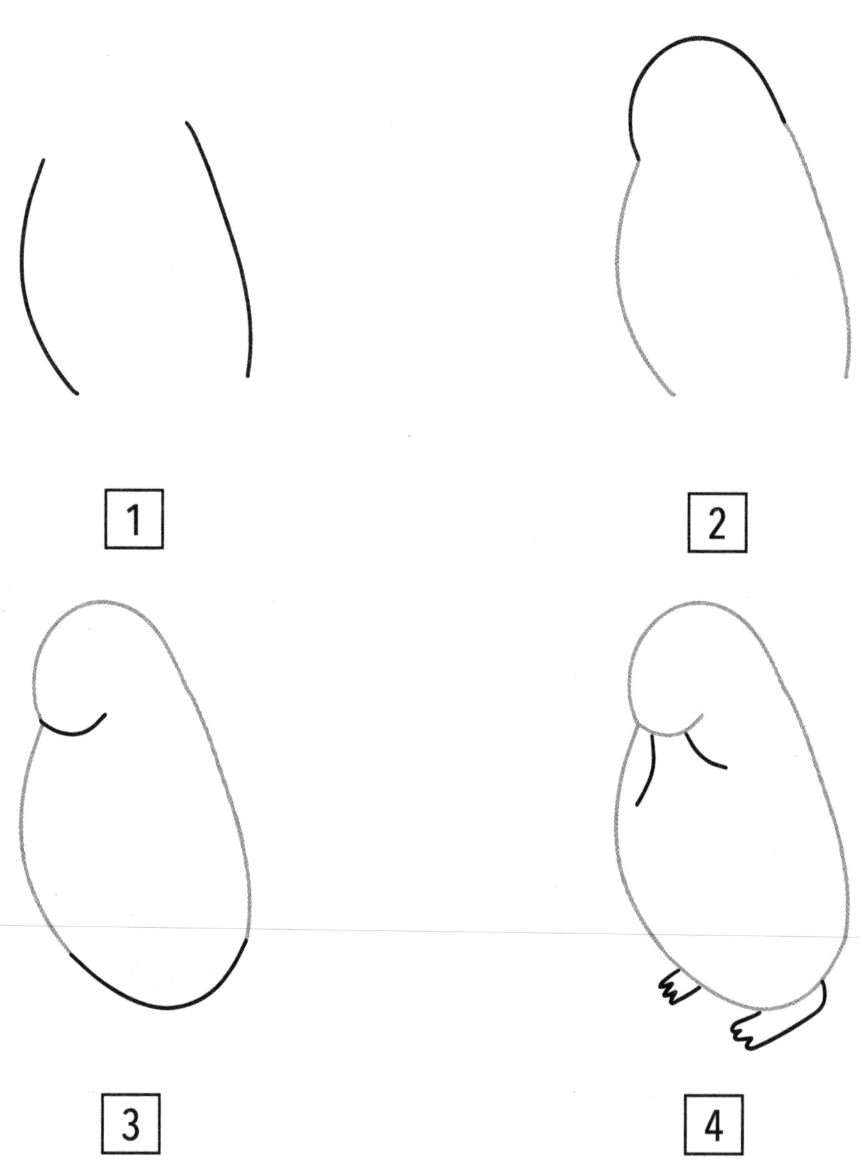

5
7

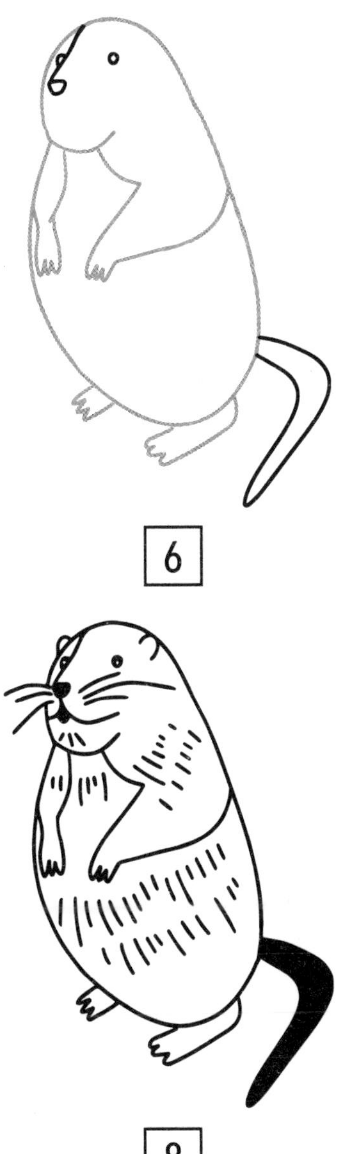
6
8

CATFISH

Have you ever wondered how the catfish got its name? Just like cats, catfish have whisker-like tendrils that help them sense their surroundings.

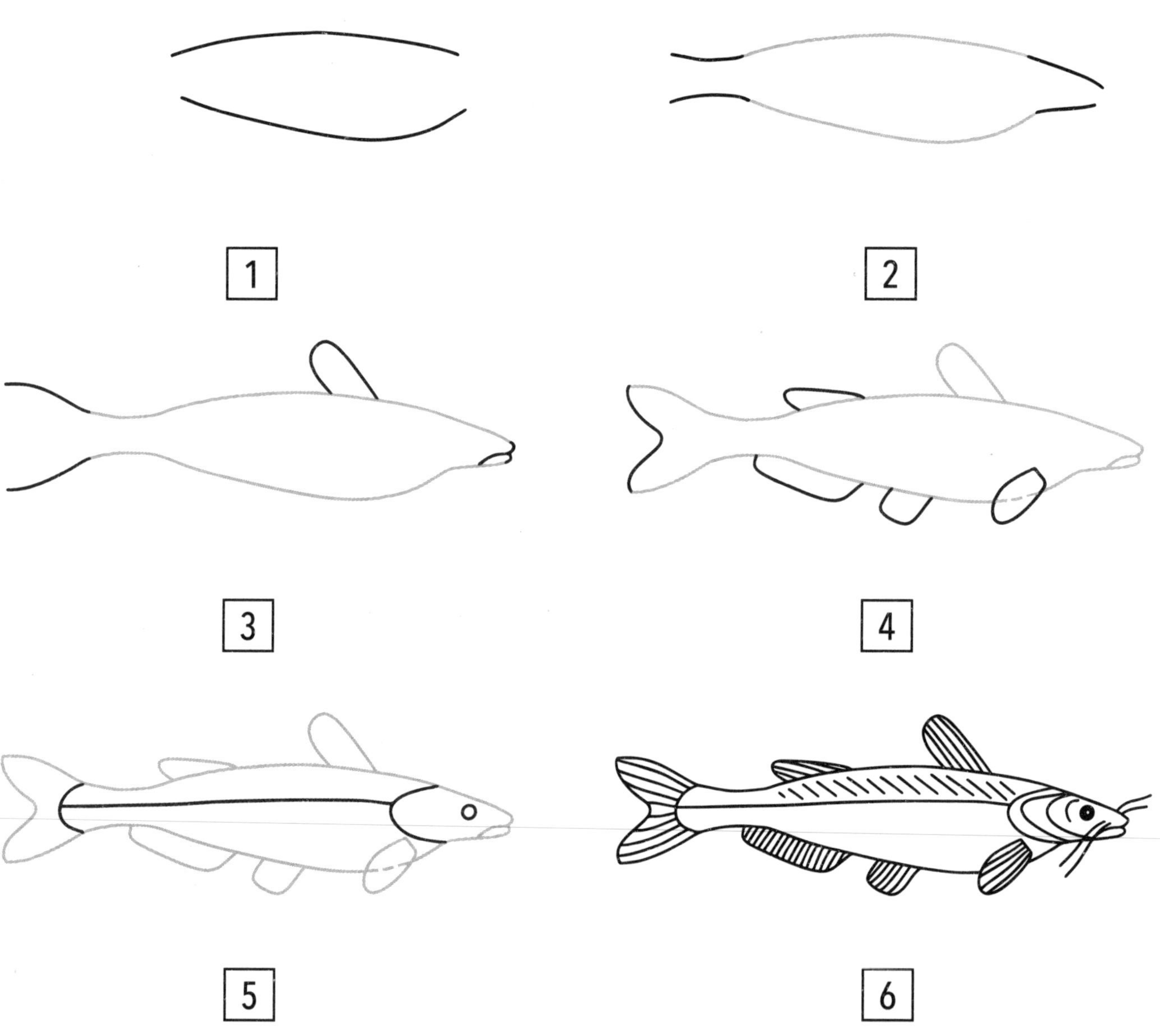

OTTER

River otters can hold their breath underwater for 8 minutes.

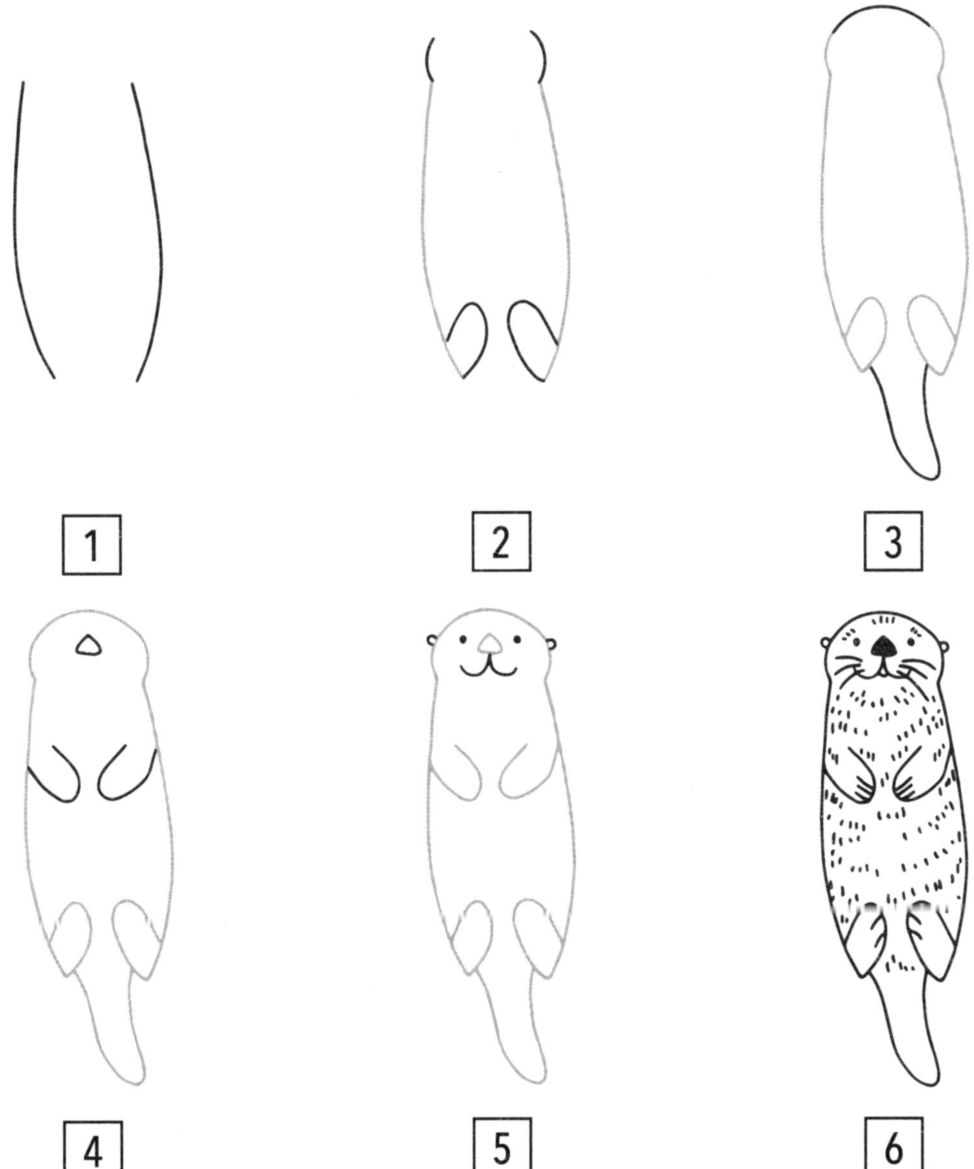

WOLF

Wolves live in groups known as wolf packs. Each pack usually consists of 5–8 wolves.

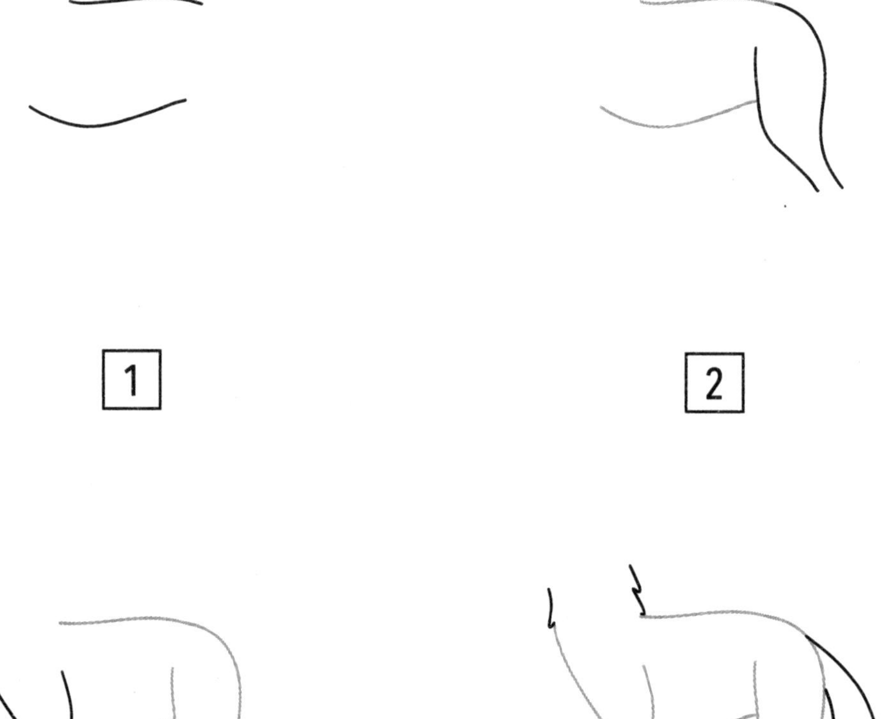

5

7

8

ANT

Ants live on every continent except Antarctica.

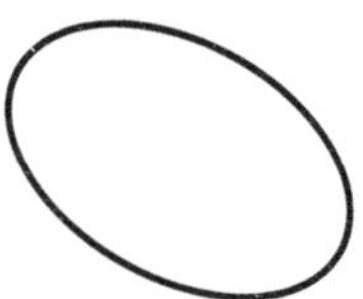

1

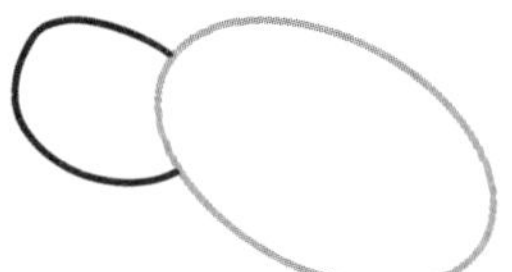

2

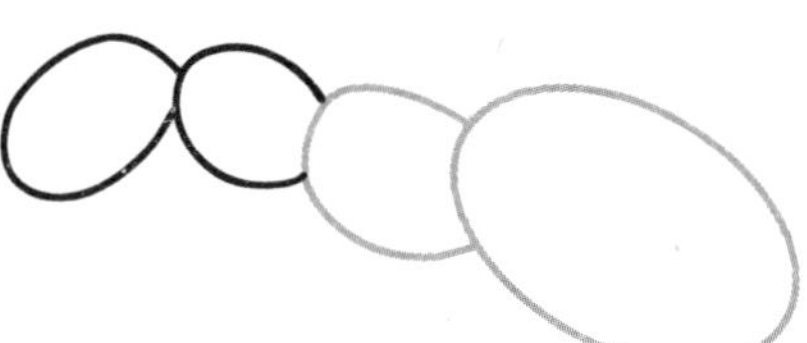

3

4

5

6

7

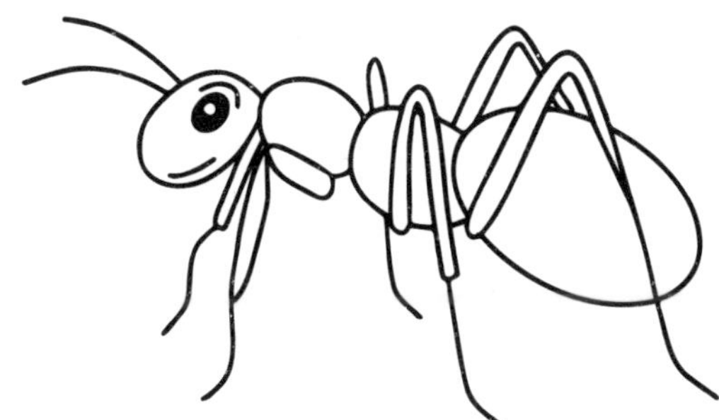

8

ROLY-POLY

Roly-polies are actually crustaceans! They're more closely related to lobsters and crabs than to the insects you find in your backyard.

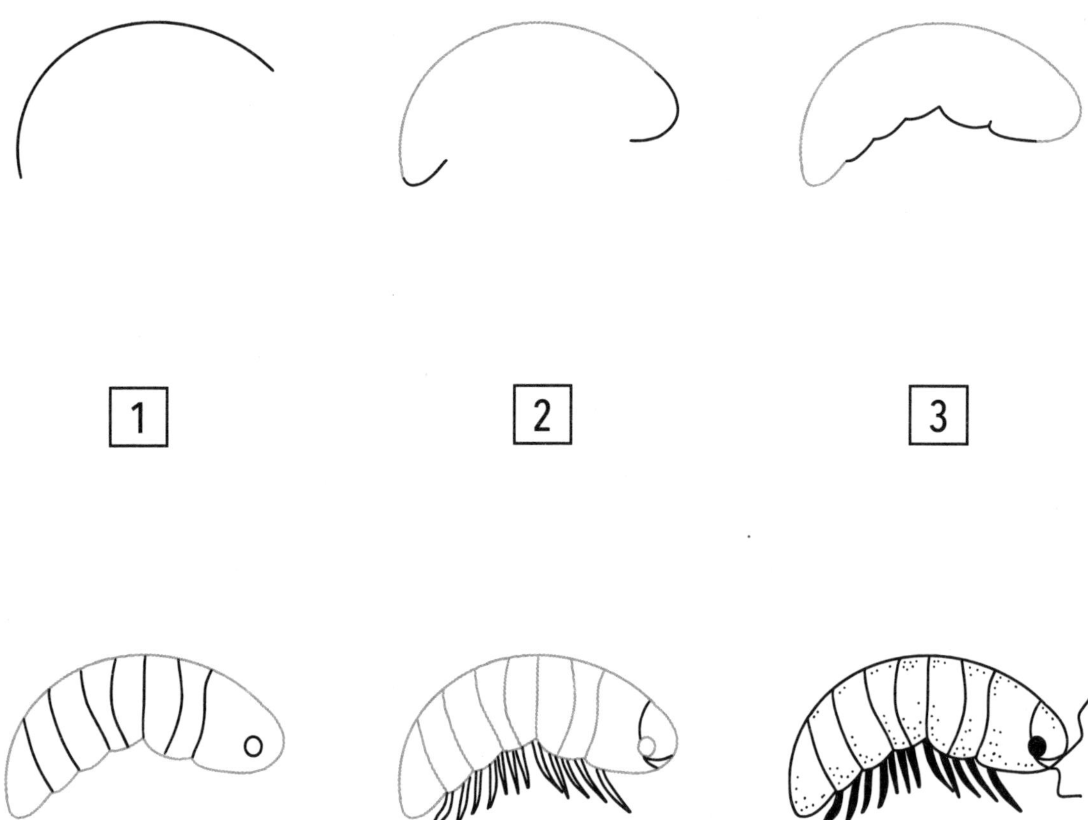

BEE

Bees have two stomachs—one for eating and the other for storing nectar, which they then use to make honey!

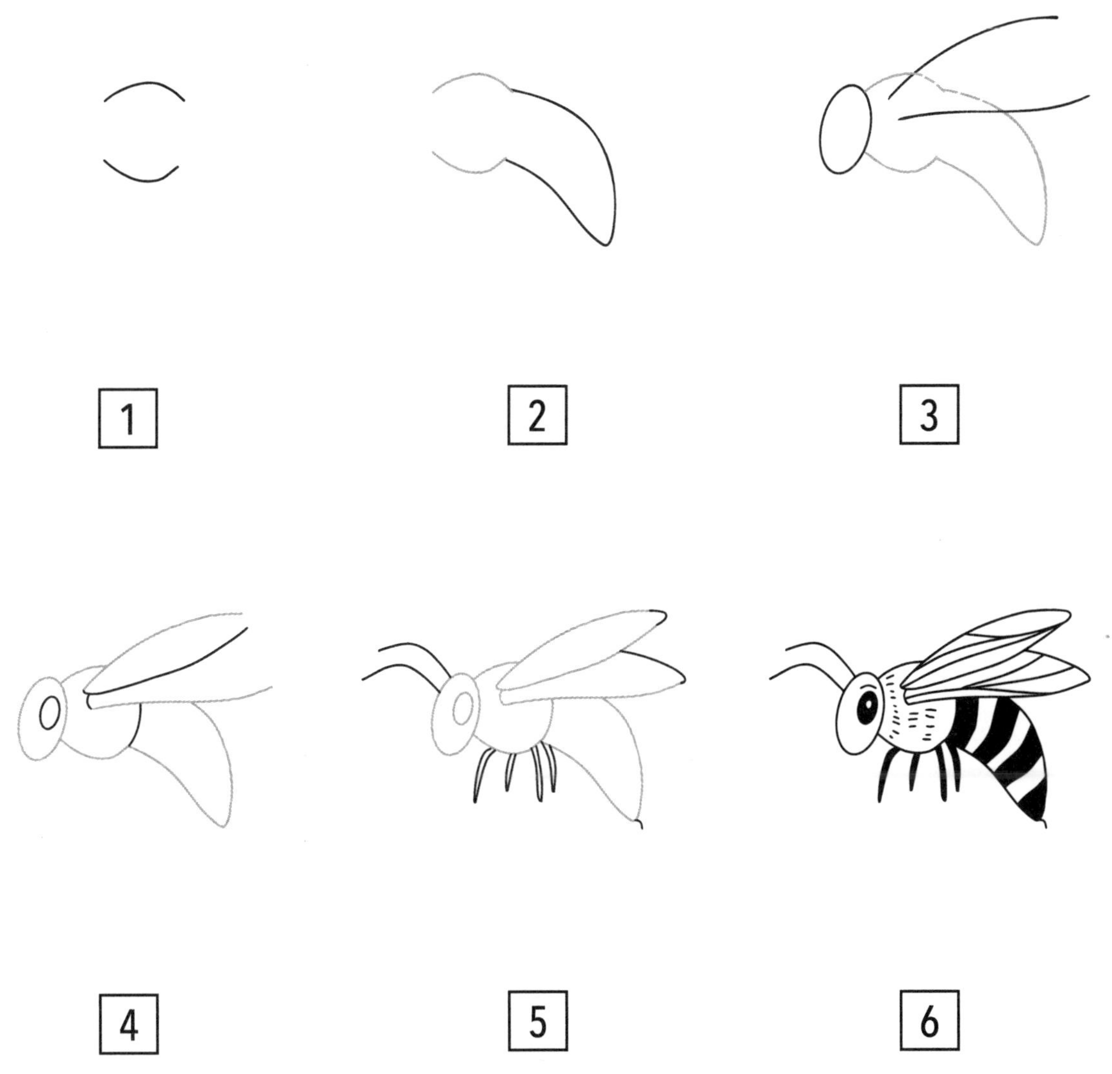

FLYING SQUIRREL

Flying squirrels can't technically fly, but they can use their wings to glide 300 feet.

5

6

7

8

MOTH

Not all moths are gray or brown! Some are green, pink, or red.

What color will your moth be?

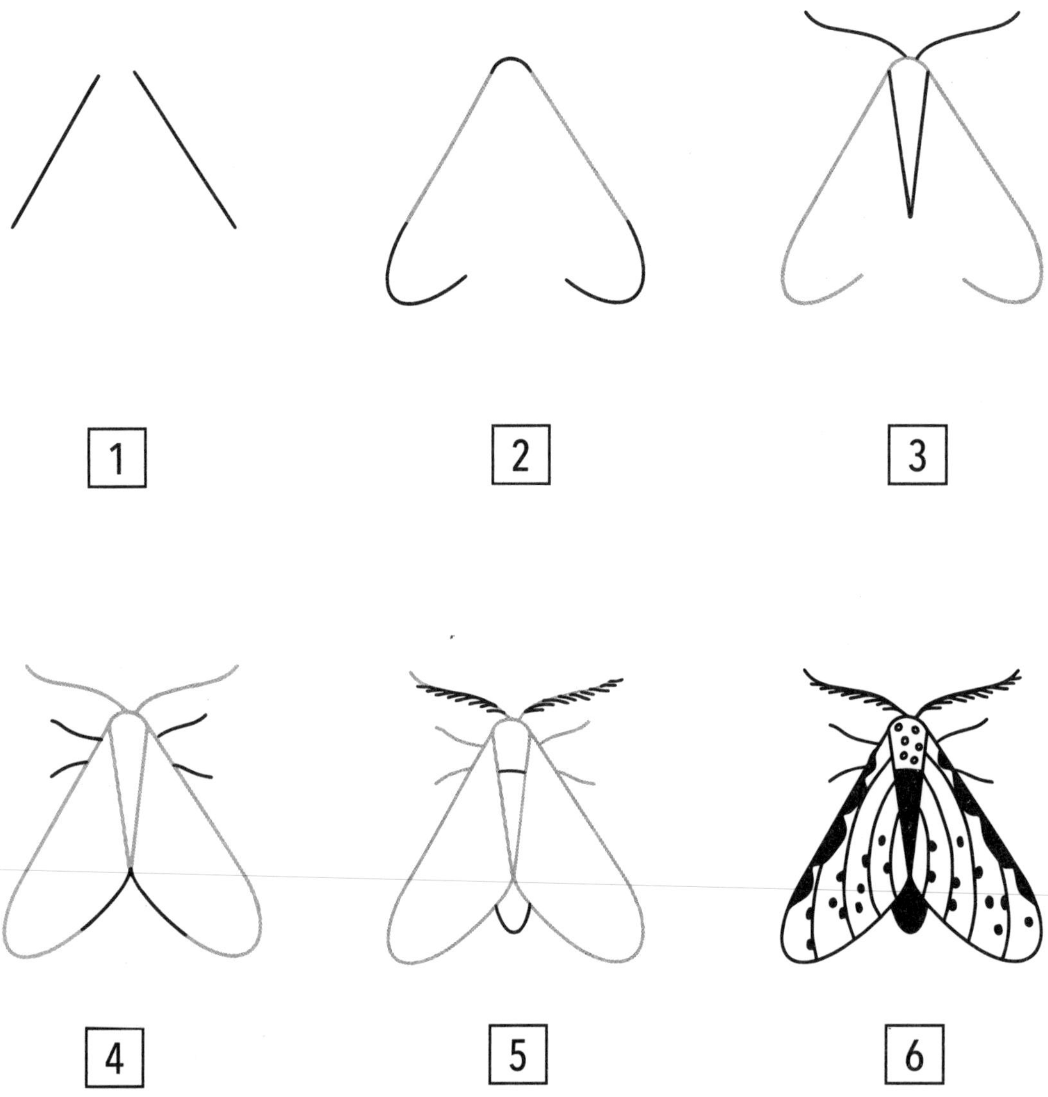

OWL

Owls can't move their eyes, but they can rotate their heads 270° to see behind them.

HAWK

Some hawks can fly more than 150 miles per hour.

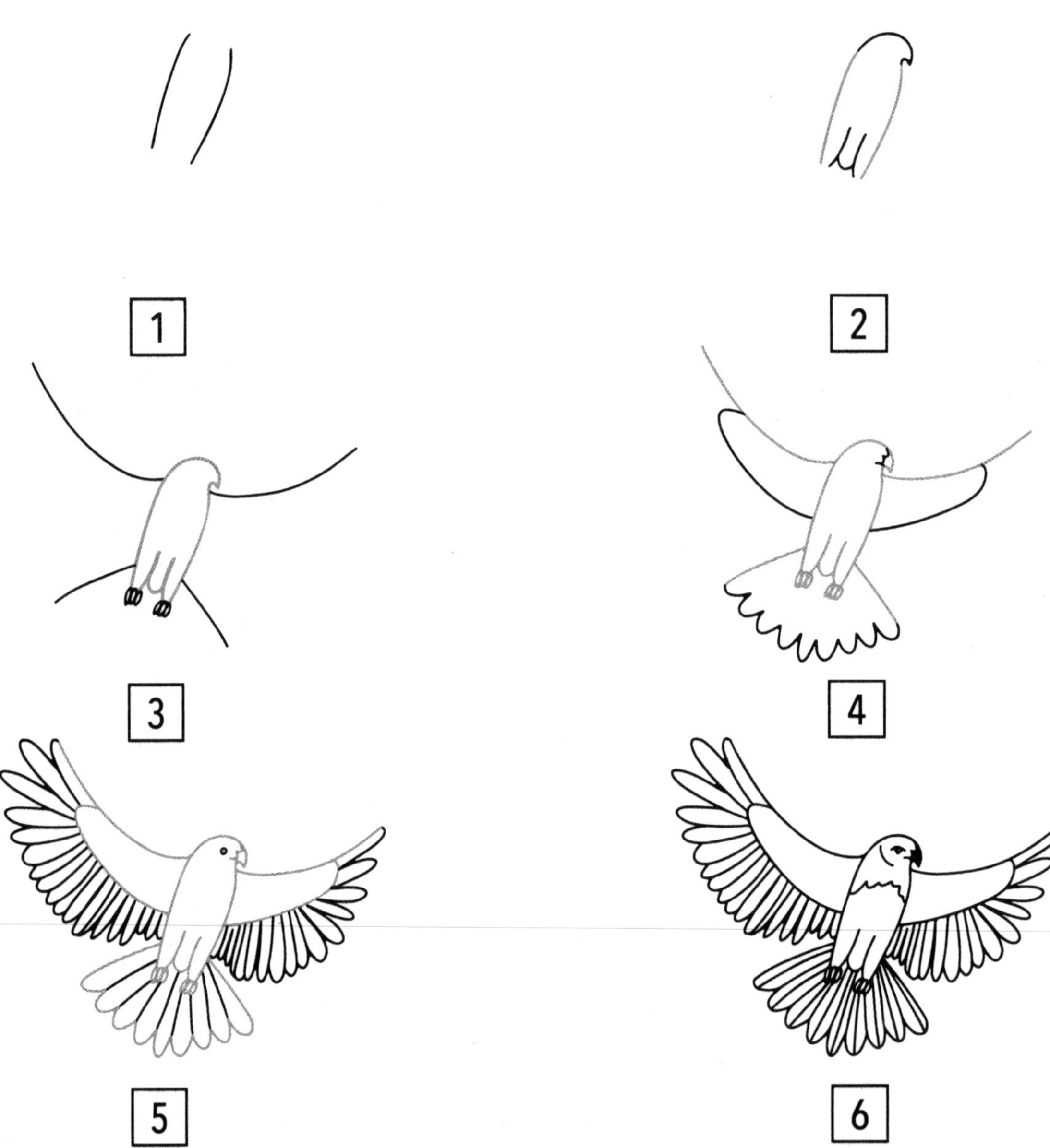

WOODPECKER

Woodpeckers have sticky tongues, which help them pull out insects from the holes they peck into trees.

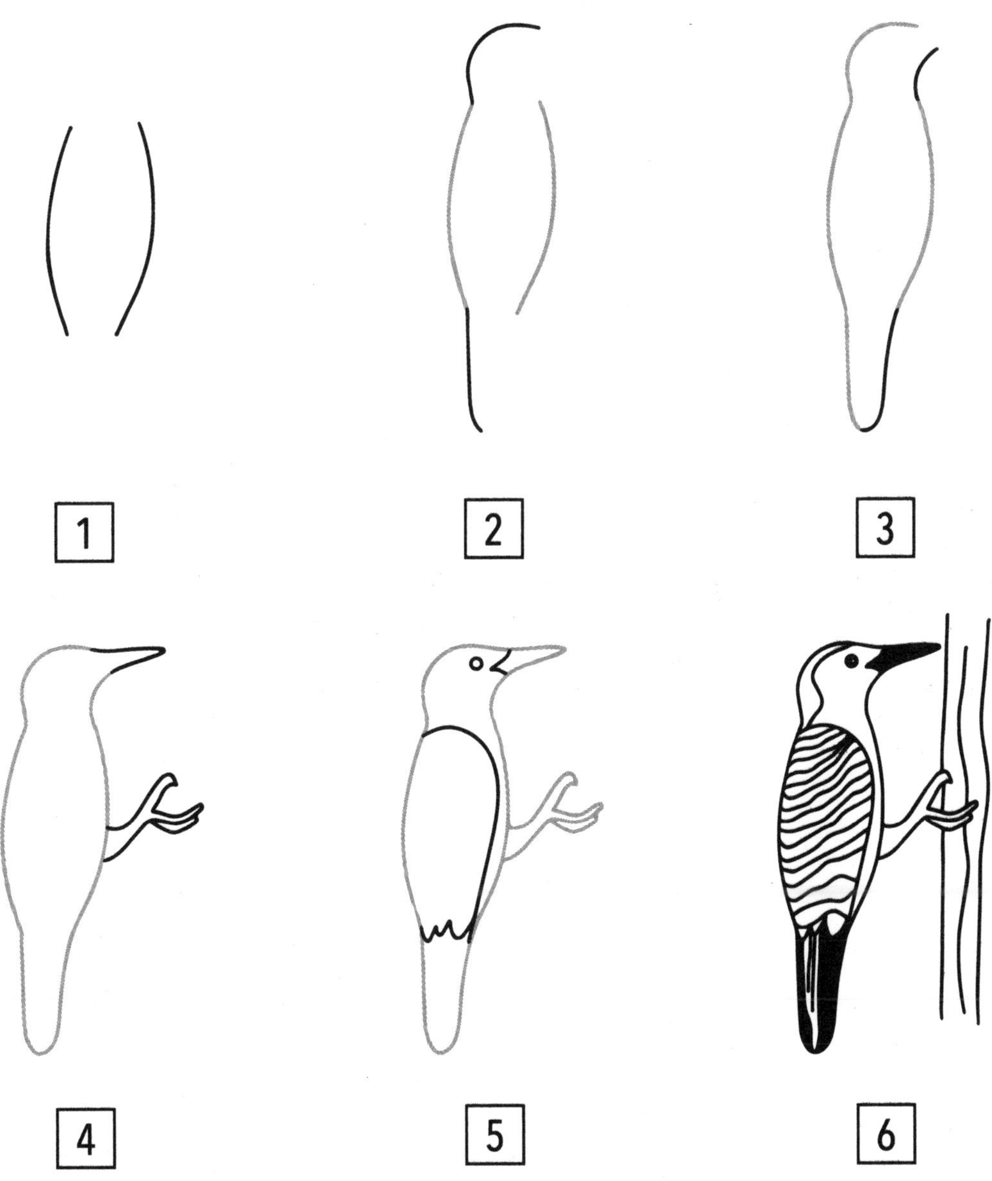

SONGBIRD

There are more than 4,000 species of songbirds, and each species has its own unique song.

LARK

Larks live in a wide range of habitats, from hot deserts to cold alpine tundras.

BAT

Bats are the only mammals that fly.

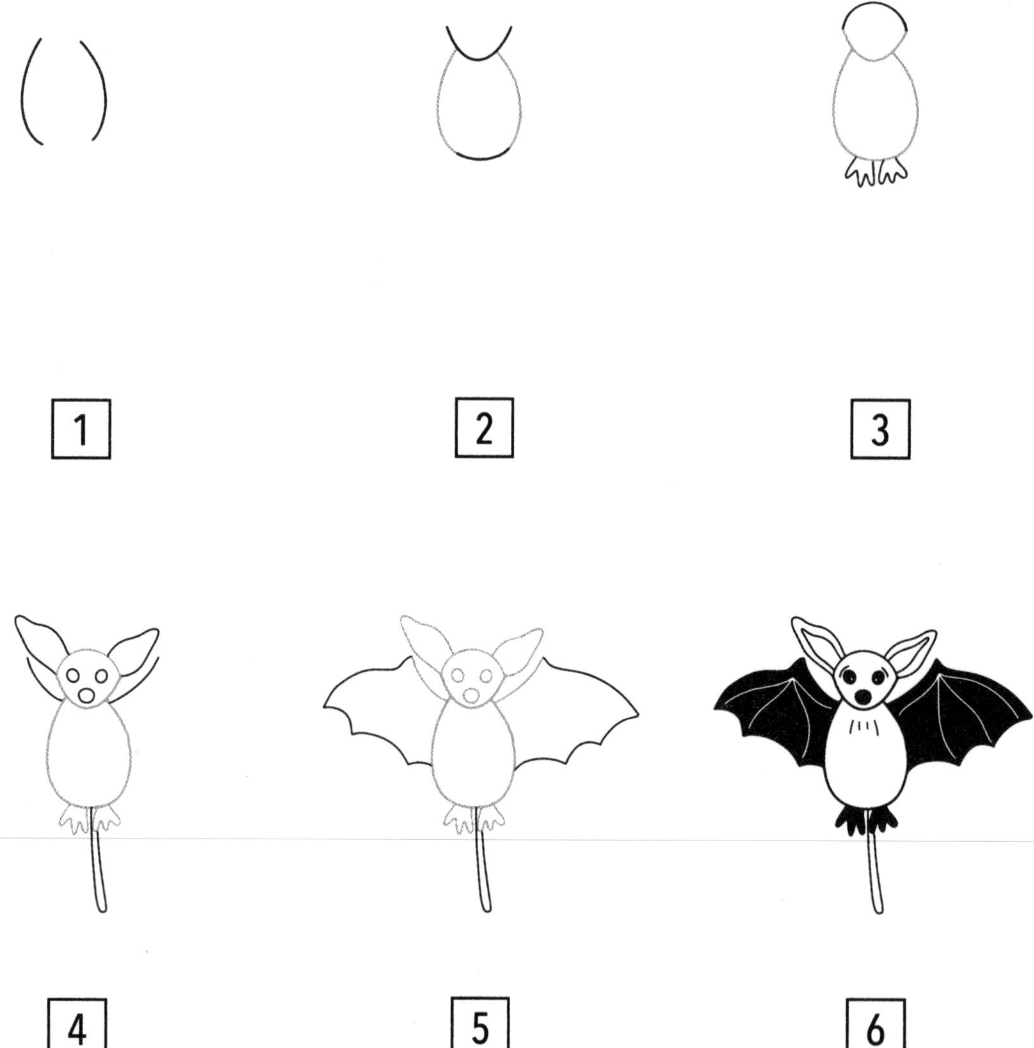

MOCKINGBIRD

If you hear a mockingbird sing, it's probably a male. Female mockingbirds only sing when they're setting up their territory for the winter.

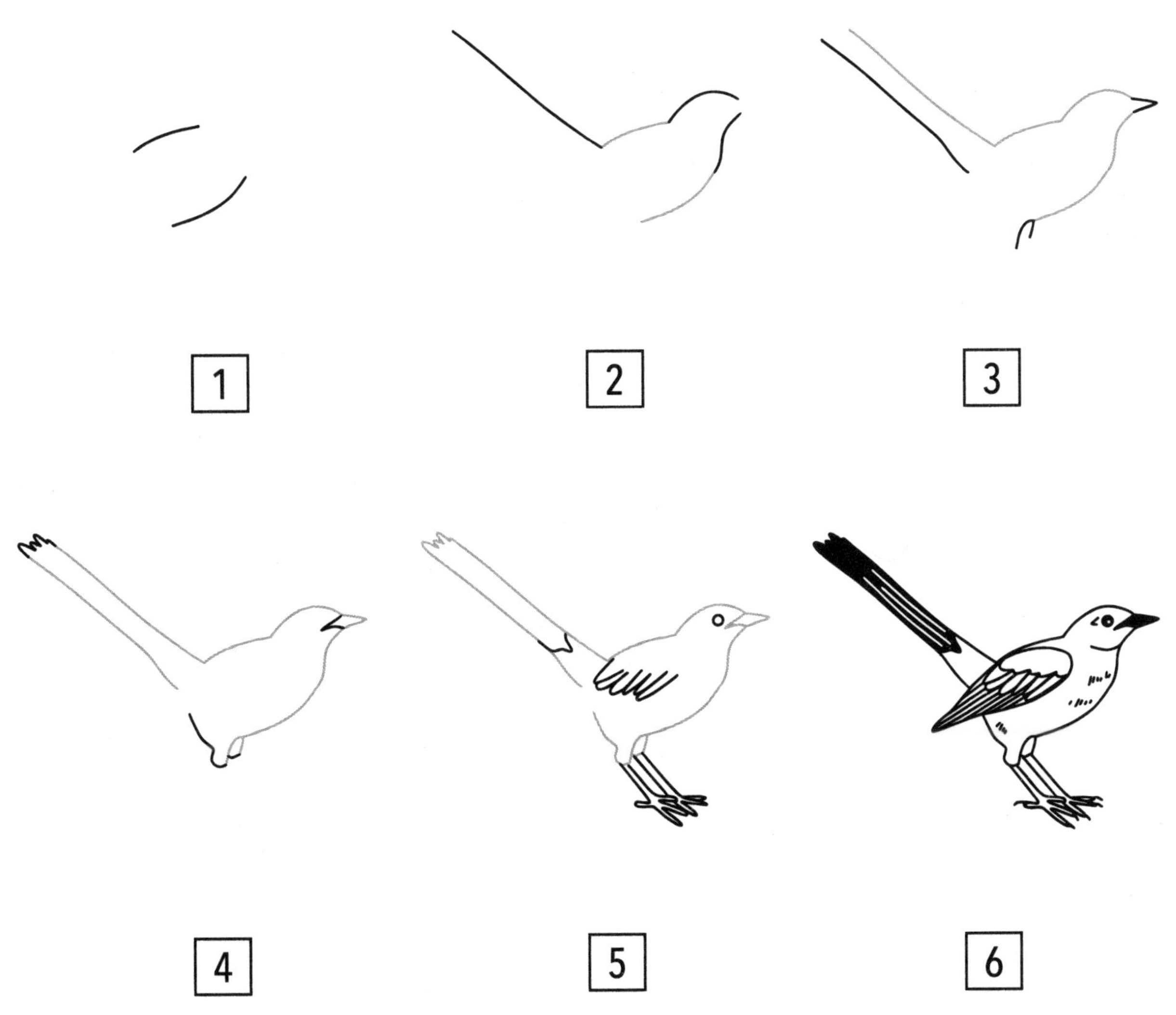

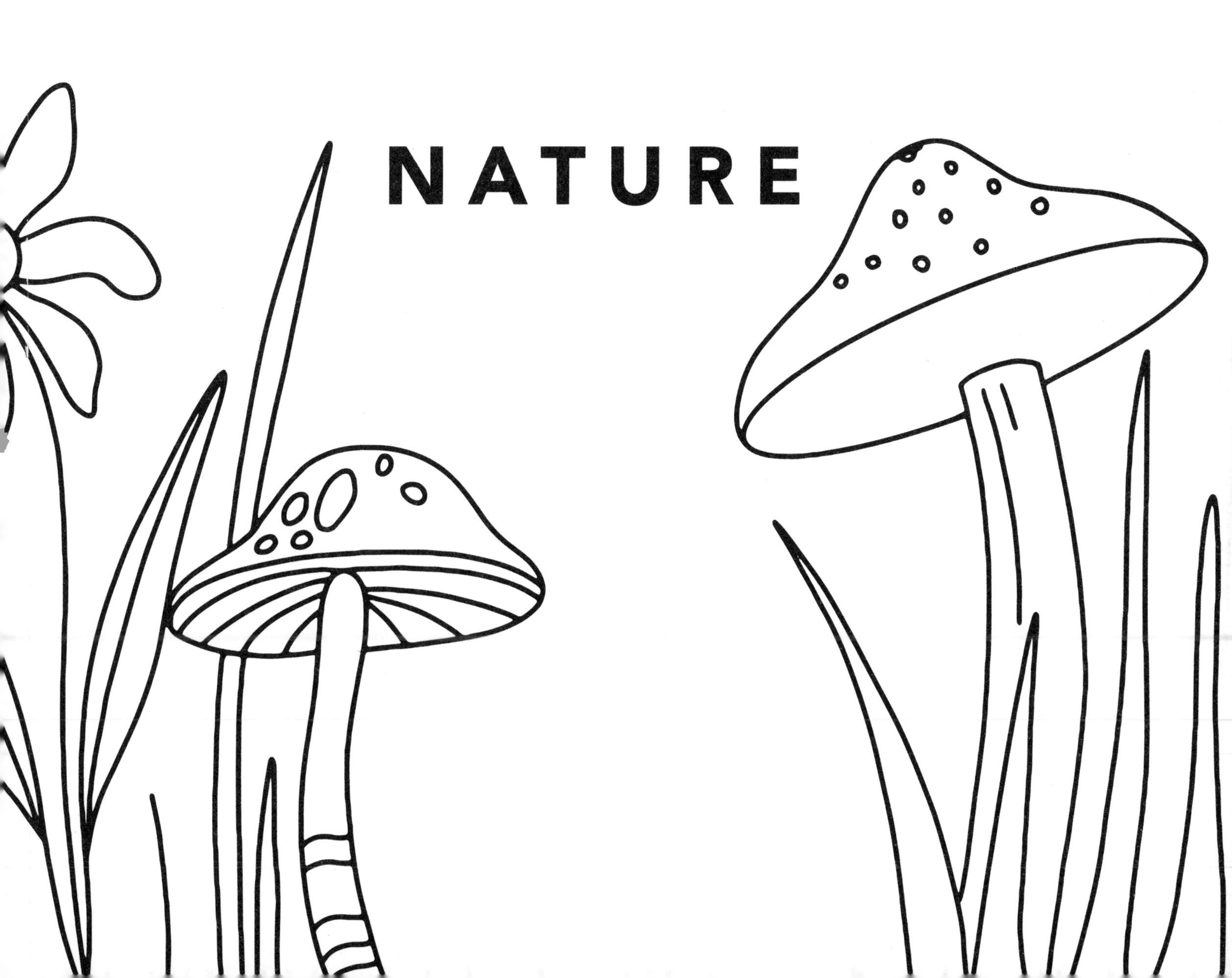
NATURE

FERN

Scientists have discovered ferns in fossils that are more than 180 million years old.

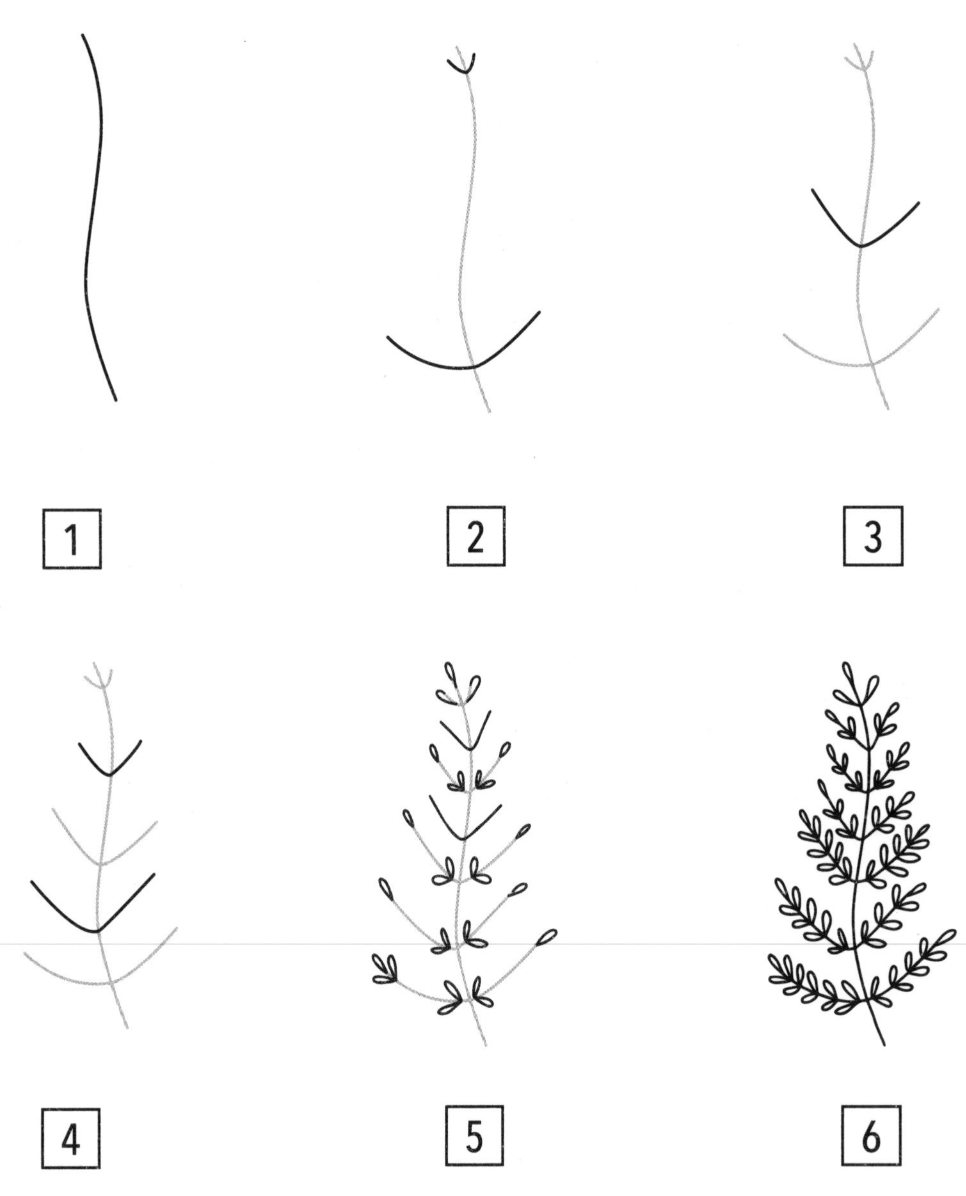

FOUR-LEAF CLOVER

There's a 1 in 10,000 chance that you'll find a lucky four-leaf clover.

1

2

3

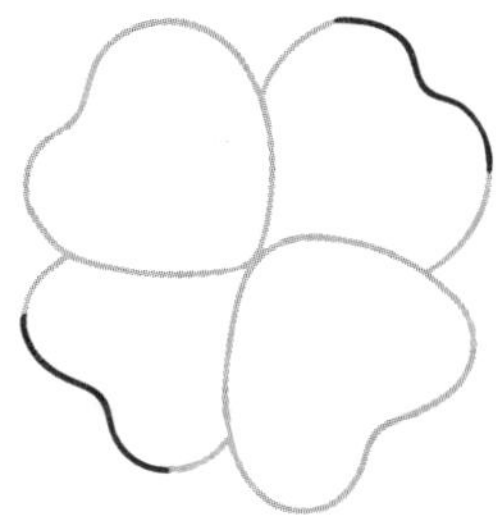

4

5

6

DECIDUOUS TREE

The average tree produces nearly 260 pounds of oxygen each year, which is enough for two people for the year!

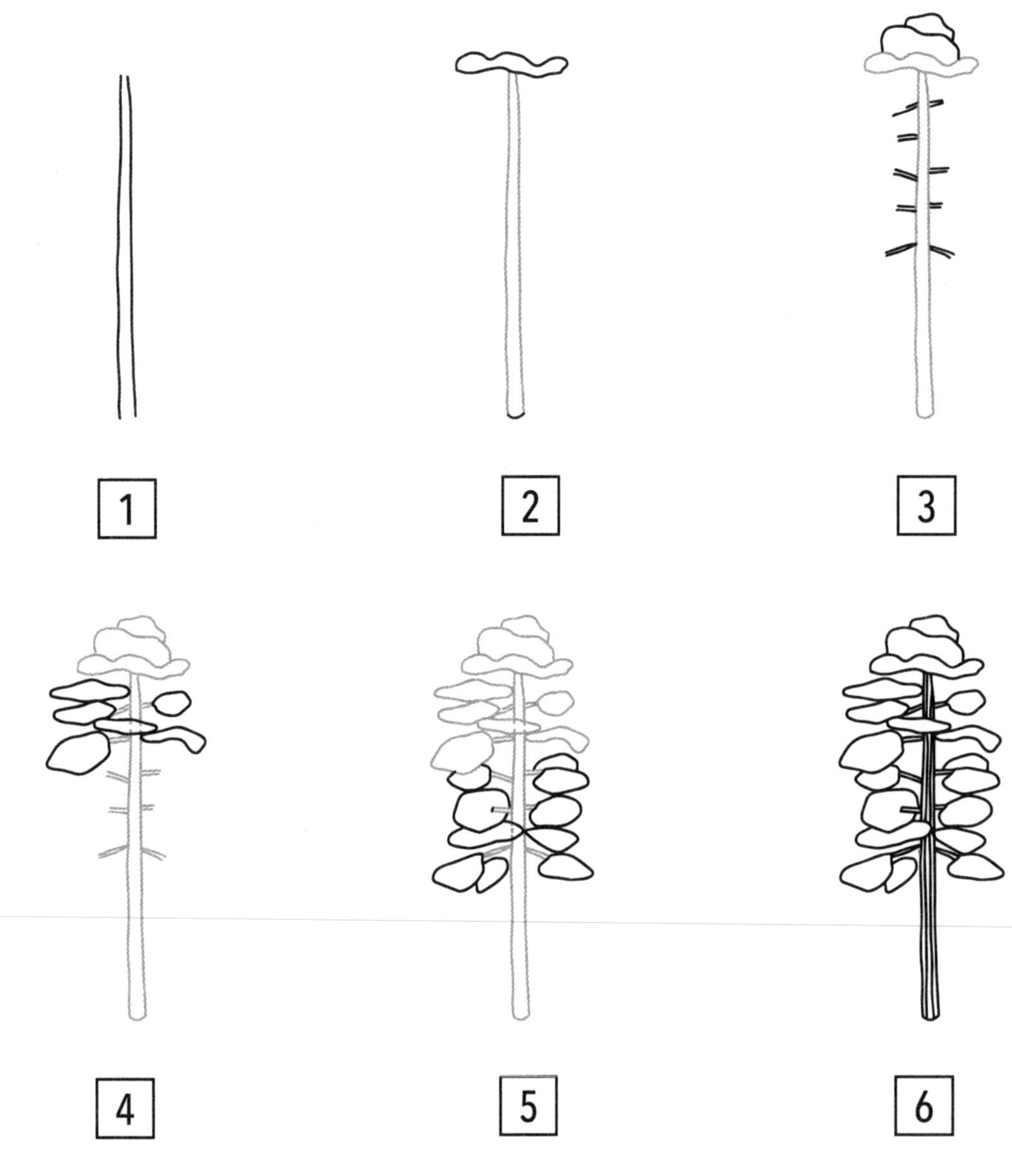

EVERGREEN TREE

Unlike deciduous trees, evergreen trees keep their leaves and stay green all year long.

WILDFLOWER

Wildflowers are flowers that can grow in the wild, without any help from humans.

PINE CONE

Did you know that pine cones hold the seeds of the pine tree? When the weather is cold, pine cones close their scales to keep the seeds safe.

DANDELION

A dandelion's seeds can travel up to 5 miles away—which is equivalent to 88 football fields.

BLACKBERRY

Not to be confused with raspberries, blackberries start out red before they ripen and turn black.

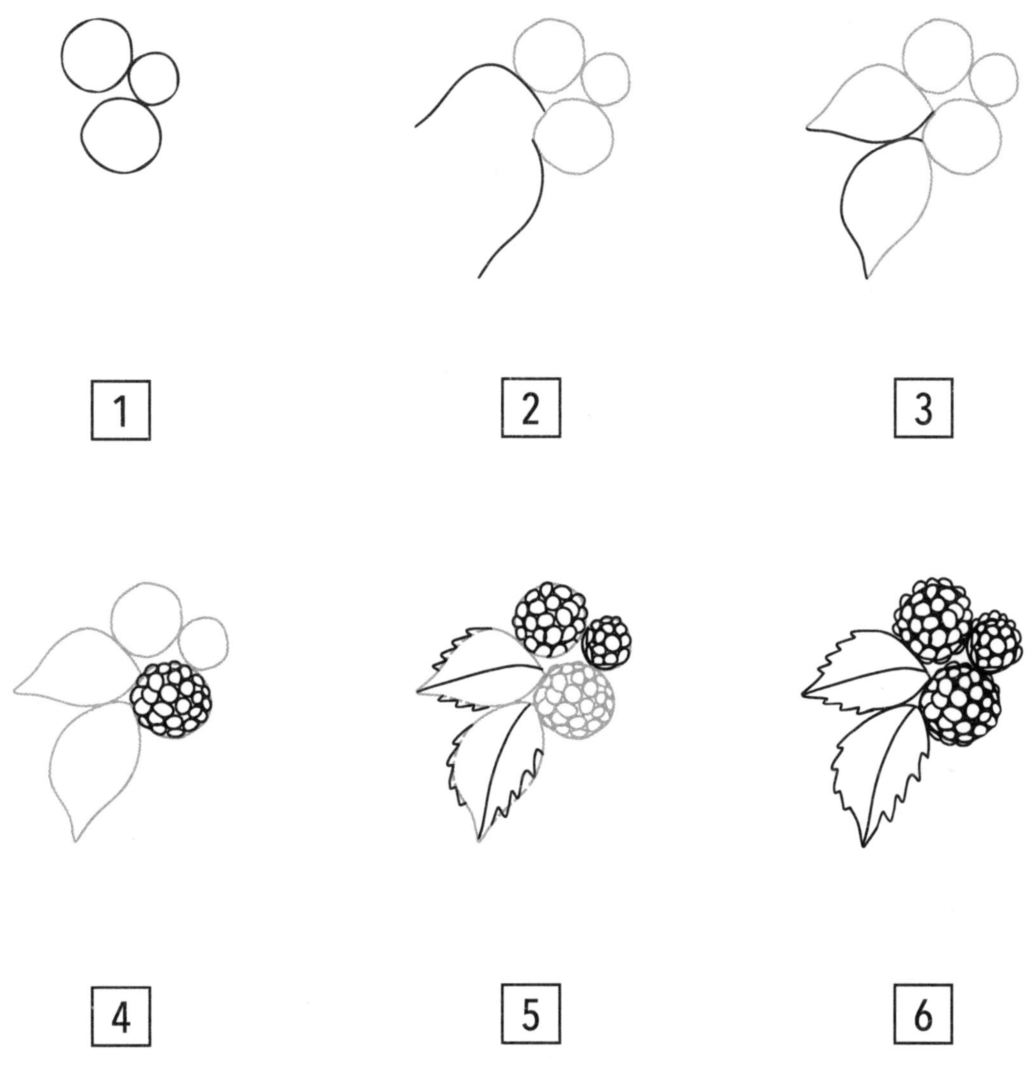

POISON IVY

Poison ivy doesn't affect most animals, only humans and some primates.

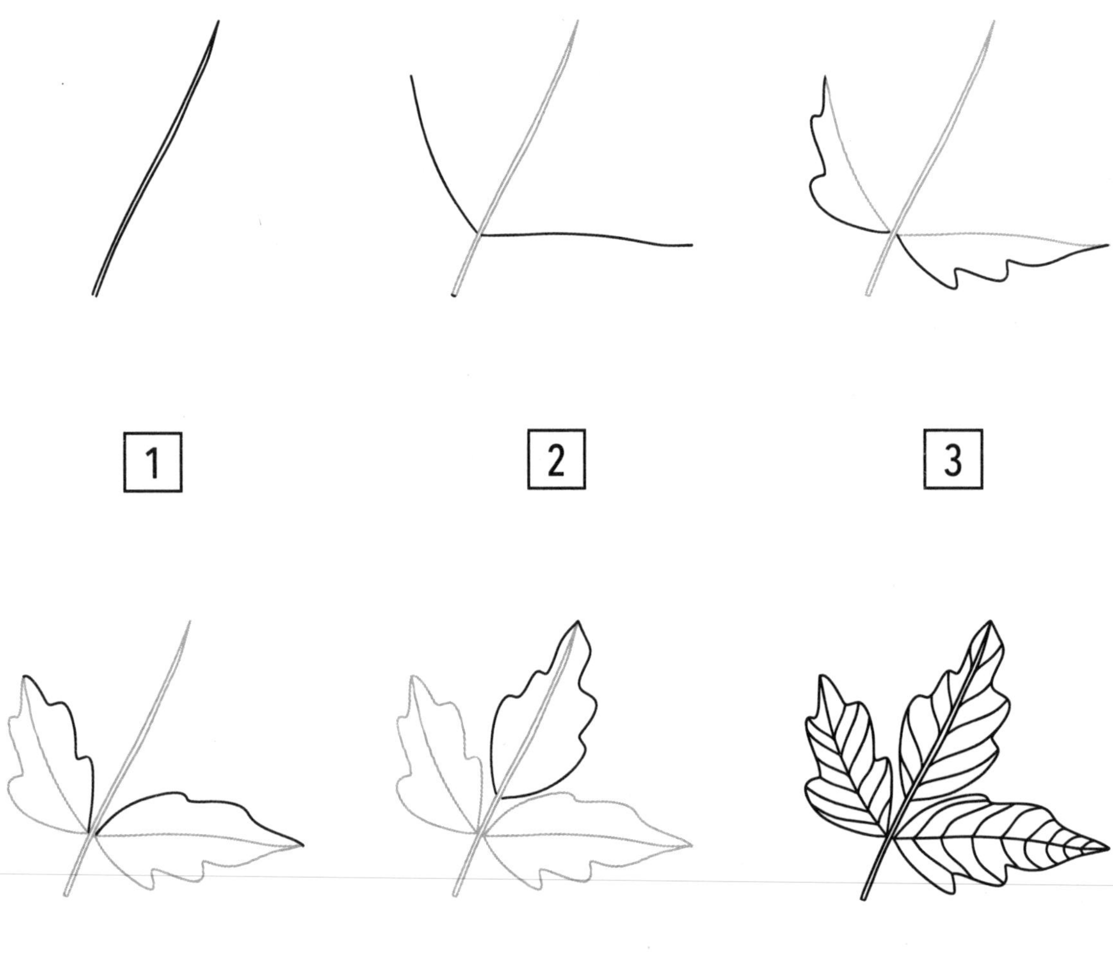

OYSTER MUSHROOM

Oyster mushrooms have a velvet-like feel and can be yellow, pink, blue, or gray.

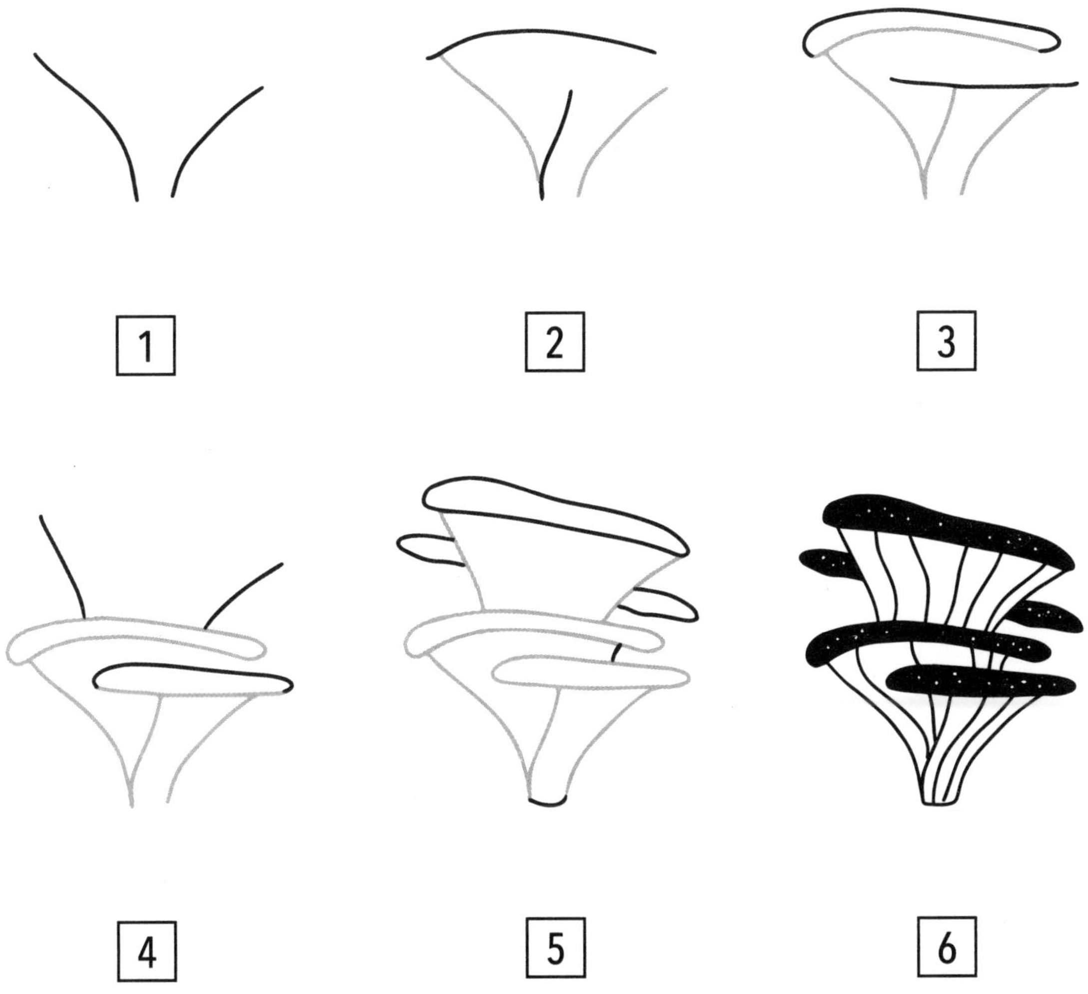

BUTTON MUSHROOM

Button mushrooms grow in damp soil, often popping up after it rains.

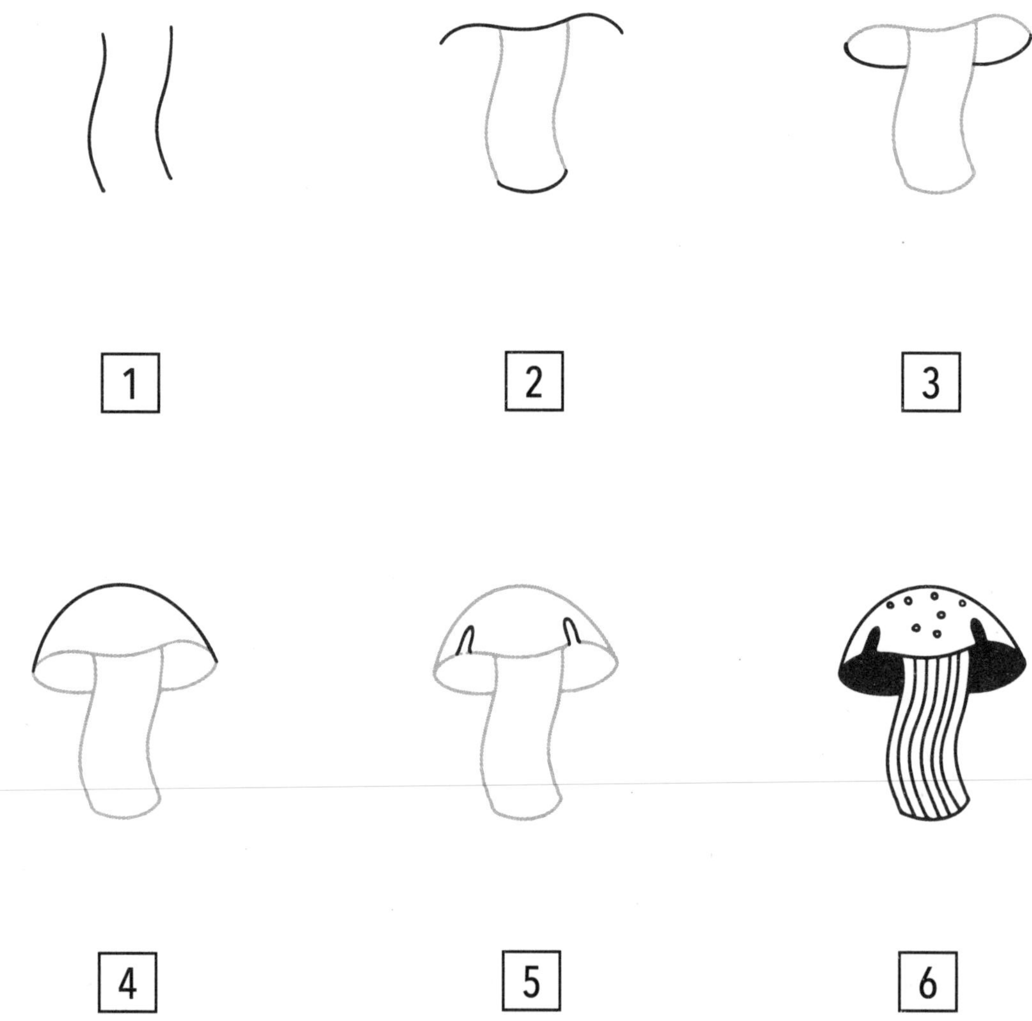

YELLOW AMERICAN BLUSHER MUSHROOM

The bumps on the Yellow American Blusher's cap are called "warts."

LAWN MOWER MUSHROOM

Lawn mower mushrooms are tiny, brownish mushrooms that are commonly found in yards.

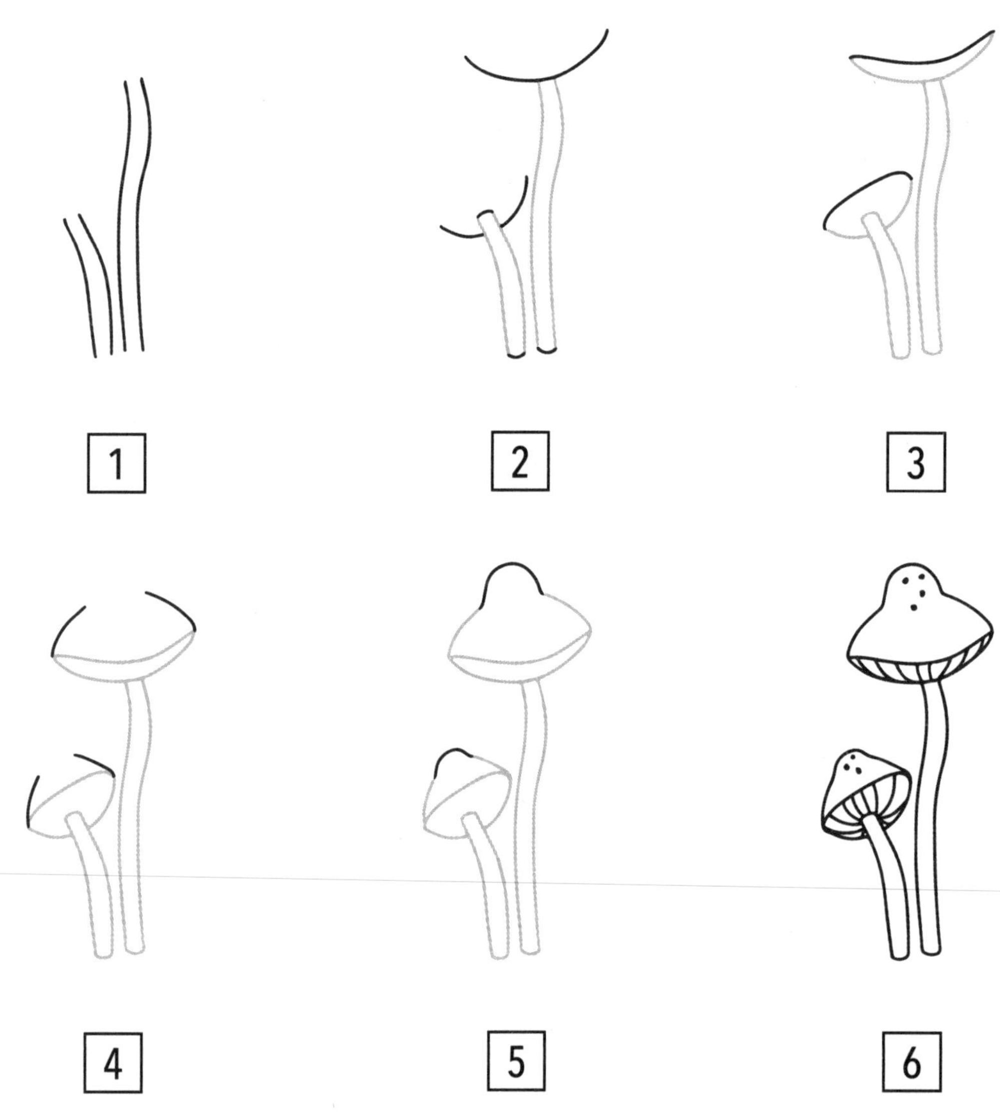

PHEASANT'S BACK MUSHROOM

The caps of pheasant's back mushrooms can grow to be a foot wide!

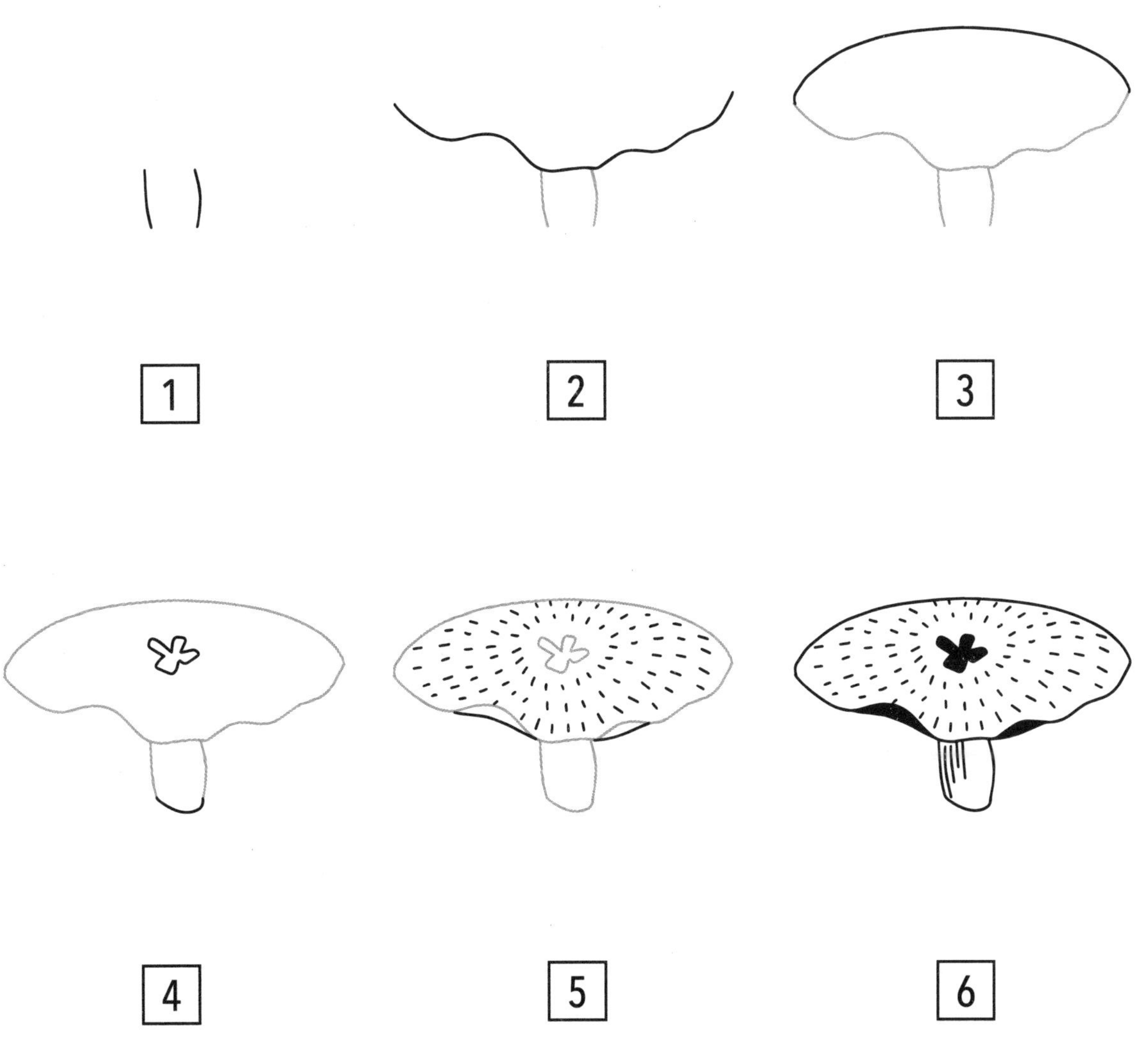

HEDGEHOG MUSHROOM

Underneath their caps, hedgehog mushrooms have hundreds of pointed spines, which look like the quills of a hedgehog!

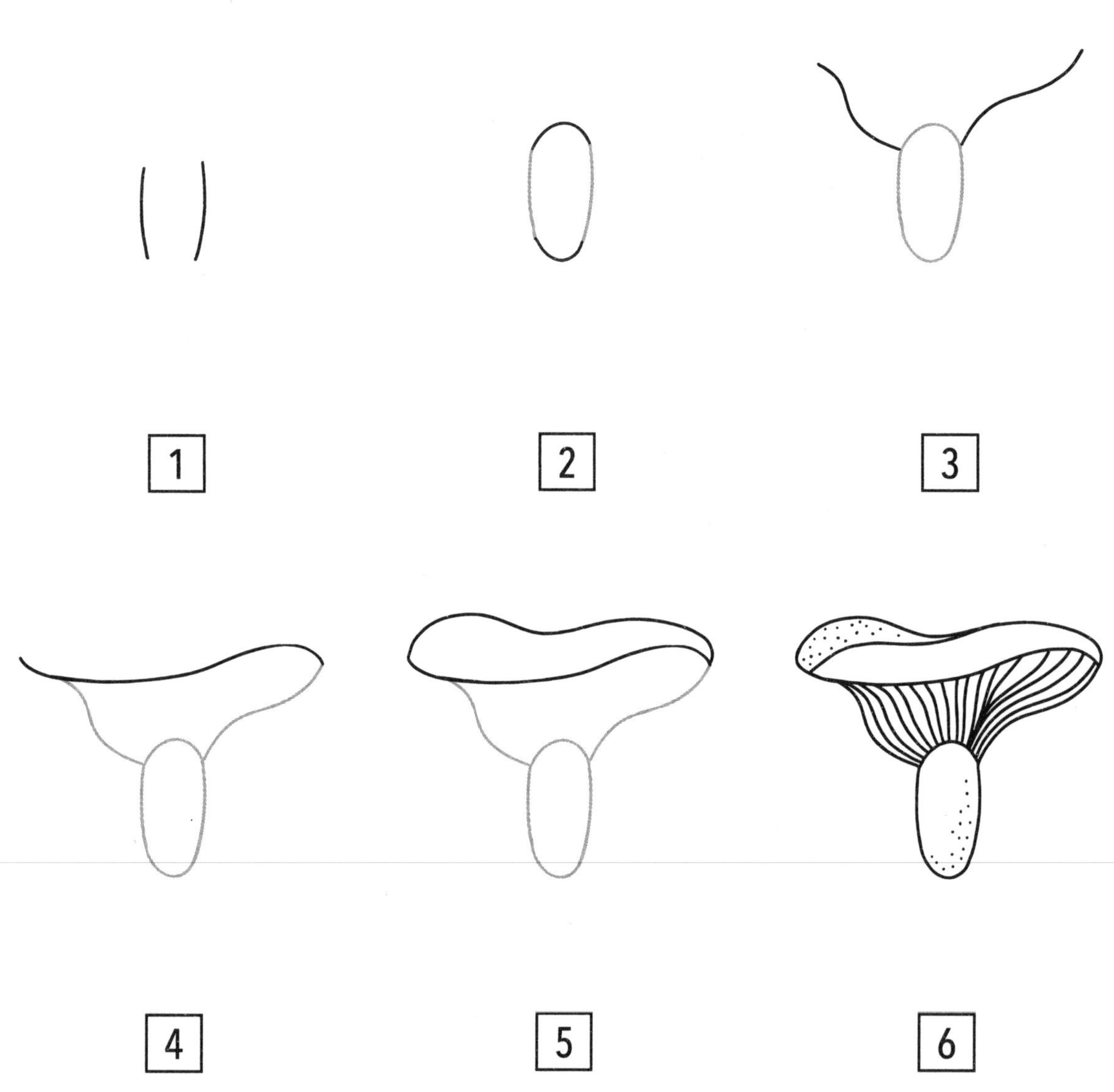

HONEY MUSHROOM

Contrary to their name, honey mushrooms aren't sweet.

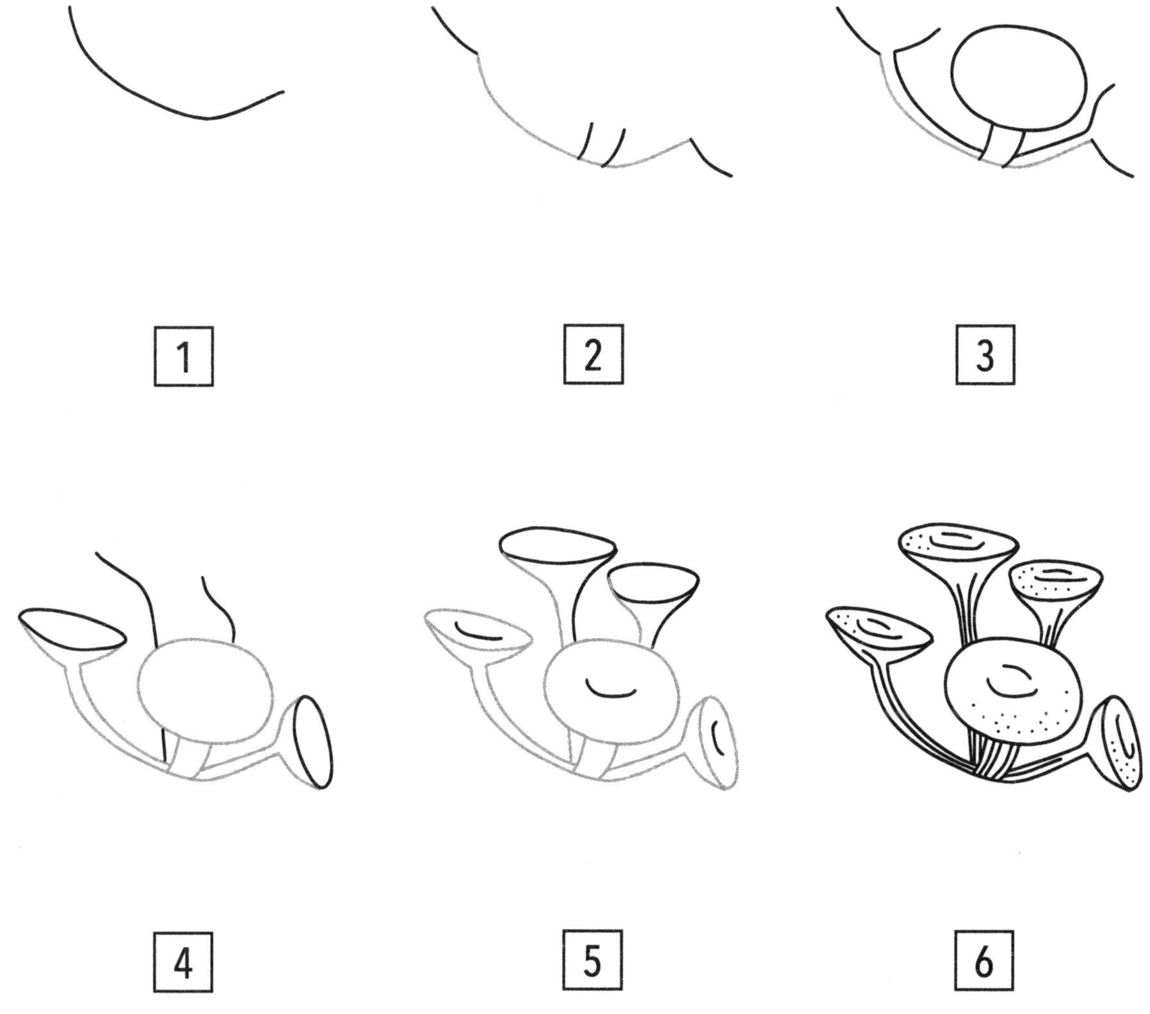

CHANTERELLE MUSHROOM

Most chanterelles are a bright, golden yellow, but some species can be white or bright red.

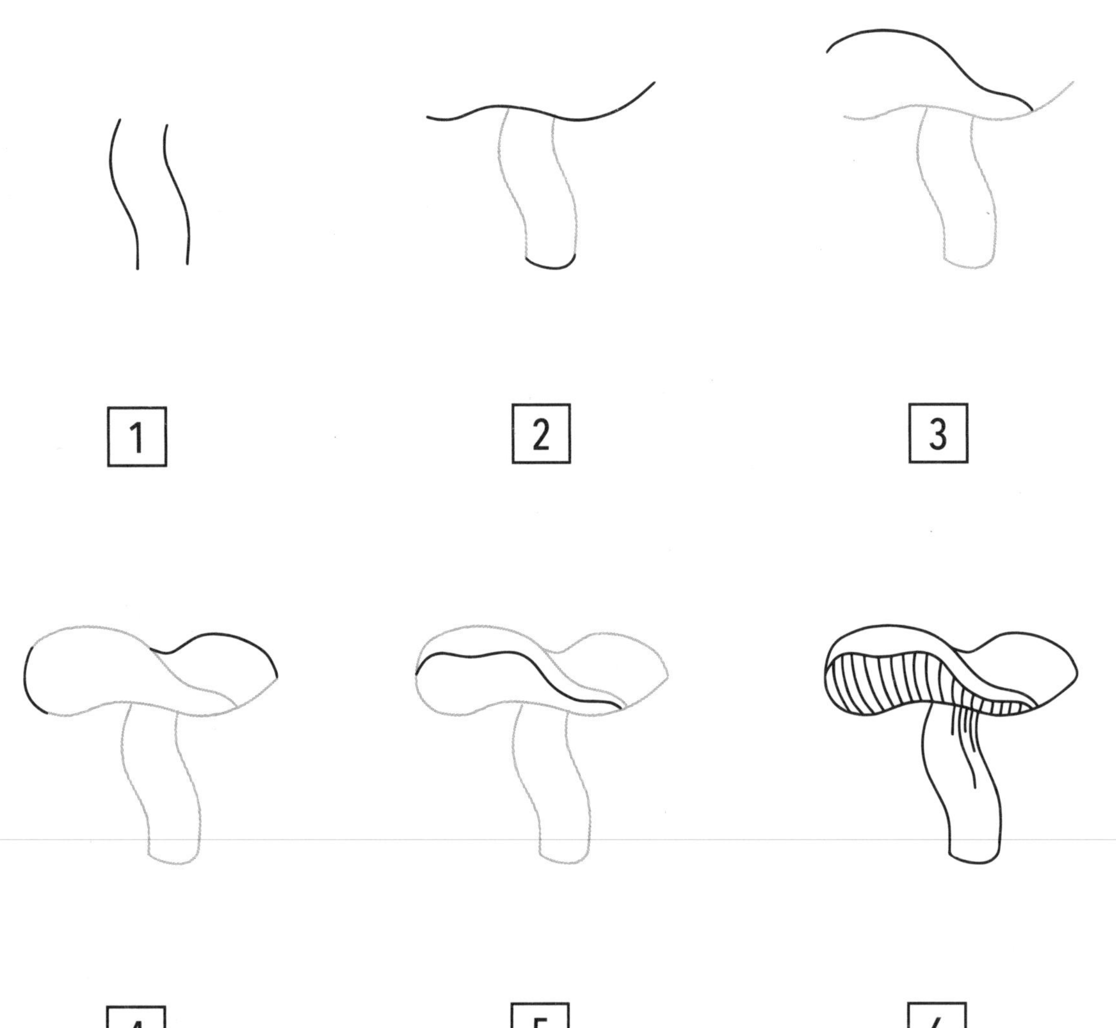

SHAGGY MANE MUSHROOM

As they mature, shaggy mane mushrooms create a black, ink-like liquid from their gills.

MILKCAP MUSHROOM

Milkcap mushrooms are bright orange but can turn green when damaged.

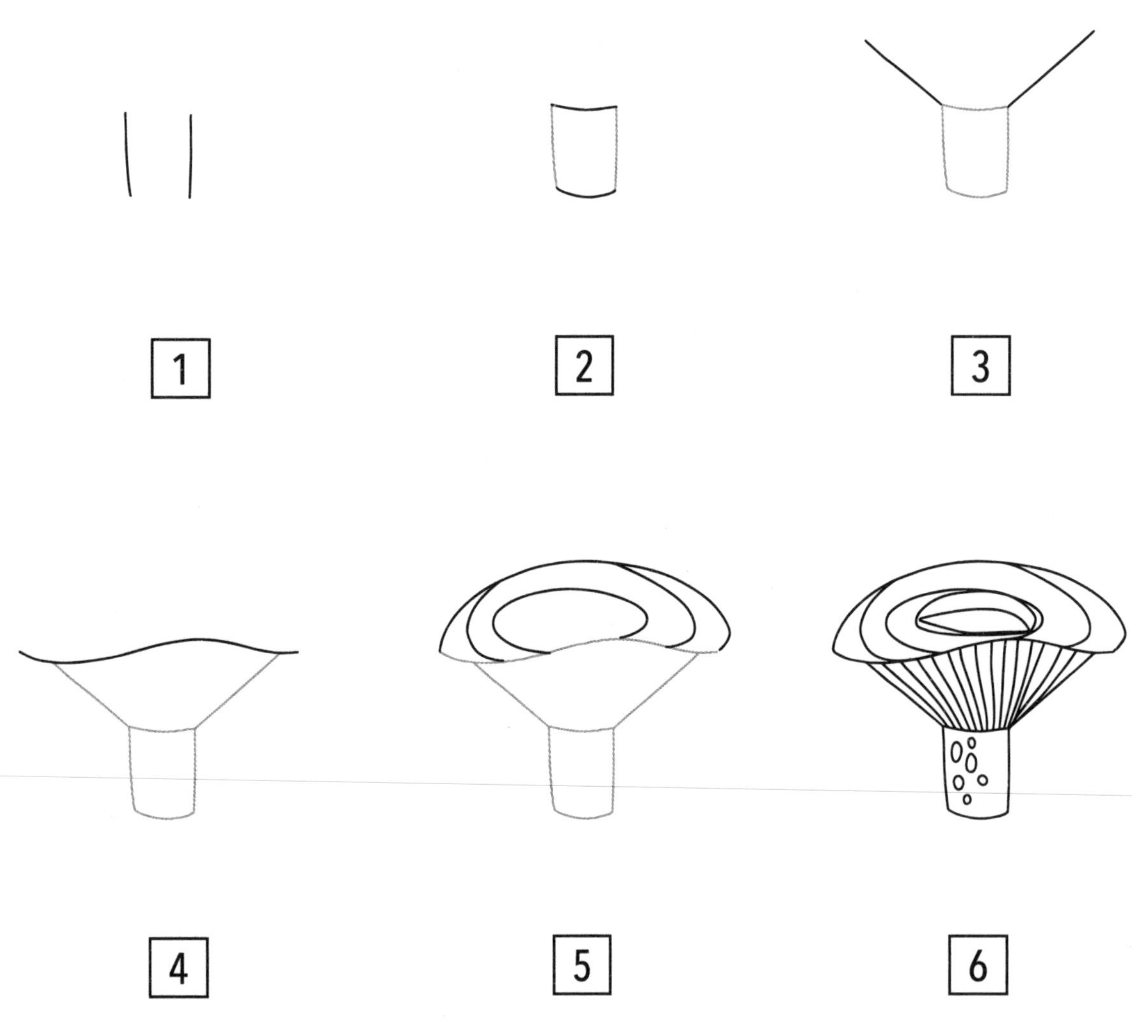

MOREL MUSHROOM

Morels come in many colors, but the most common colors are yellow, black, and white.

BEECH MUSHROOM

Beech mushrooms grow on beech trees in big clusters, which are also called "bouquets."

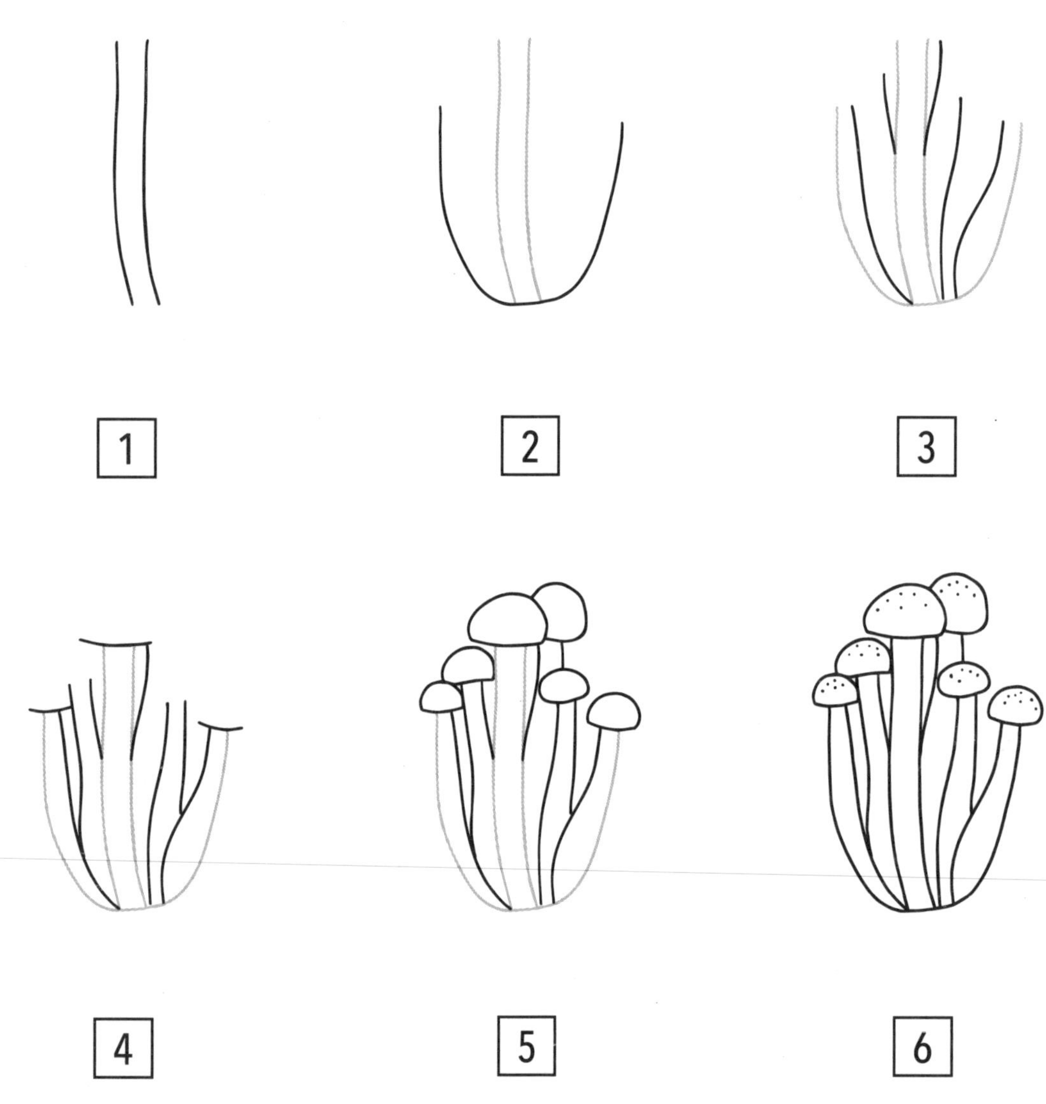

MYTHICAL FAIRY HOUSE MUSHROOM

In mythology, mushrooms can be considered symbols of luck and good fortune.

About Alli K

NAME: Alli Koch

HOME: Dallas, Texas

BIRTHDAY: March 20, 1991

FAVORITE COLOR: Black

FAVORITE FOOD: Waffle fries and fruit

JOB: I am a full-time artist! I sell my art online, paint on the side of buildings, write books, and teach others how to draw or be creative.

FAVORITE THING: A warm blanket

PETS: I have one cat named Emmie

CAR: Two-door black Jeep

FAMILY: Married to my high school sweetheart

FAVORITE ANIMALS: Cats and dolphins

FAVORITE PASTIME: Playing board games!